D0392436

THE
DEVELOPMENT
OF RURAL
AMERICA

THE
DEVELOPMENT
OF RURAL
AMERICA

Edited by

GEORGE BRINKMAN

THE UNIVERSITY PRESS OF KANSAS
Lawrence/Manhattan/Wichita

HN
65
.B72

© 1974 by the University Press of Kansas
Printed in the United States of America
Designed by Fritz Reiber

Library of Congress Cataloging in Publication Data

Brinkman, George Loris.
    The development of rural America.

    Based upon a series of seminars presented to
        the Dept. of Economics, Kansas State University
        from January to April 1971.
    1. United States—Rural conditions.
    2. Community development—United States. I. Title.
HN65.B72   301.35'0973.   73-19822
ISBN 0-7006-0112-0.

Preface

The Development of Rural America is the outgrowth of a series of seminars in rural community development presented by prominent guest speakers to the Department of Economics at Kansas State University from January to April 1971. These presentations were utilized as an integral part of a course in rural community development being taught by George Brinkman, who subsequently edited the papers into their present form. This series of seminars was undertaken as part of a continuing series of guest presentations to provide students at Kansas State University with opportunities to meet, and to discuss current issues with, top professionals in economics and agricultural economics. Funding for the seminar honorariums and part of the subsequent development of the book was provided by the College of Agriculture and approved through the Office of the Vice-President for Academic Affairs.

The six guest authors—J. Carroll Bottum, Richard Hausler, Calvin Beale, Luther Tweeten, Emery Castle, and Niles M. Hansen —provided their chapters as a summary of the material that each person presented in several seminars at Kansas State University. In addition, the chapter on rural problems was added by the editor to provide a more complete presentation of rural development. The topic of rural development is very important throughout the United States, and this book should provide under one cover valuable material prepared by some of the foremost specialists in rural development.

Our appreciation is expressed to the many people involved in the development of this book. Special gratitude is expressed to the guest speakers for their presentations and to those who assisted in the preparation of the manuscripts. Appreciation is also expressed to Paul Kelley, department head, and to other faculty members of the Department of Economics for sponsoring and promoting the seminar series.

Carroll Hess
Dean of Agriculture
Kansas State University

55349

Introduction

In the last decade, rural development emerged as one of the prominent challenges facing the United States. Strong support for rural development is now found in both major political parties and at federal, state, and local levels. President Nixon gave early recognition to the urgency of rural problems and commitment to solutions for them in his first State of the Union message:

> We must create a new rural environment which will not only stem the migration to urban centers but reverse it. If we seize our growth as a challenge, we can make the 1970s a historic period when by conscious choice we transformed our land into what we want it to become.

The growing support for rural development today results in great part from the fact that despite unprecedented growth, both urban and rural areas in the United States are greatly deficient in many aspects of quality living conditions. On the one hand, the nation's cities are slowly strangling themselves, jamming together people and industry, and spawning pollution, transportation paralysis, housing blight, lack of privacy, and a crime-infested society. Rural areas simultaneously suffer from the other extreme—lack of sufficient employment opportunities, outmigration and depopulation, and too few people to support services and institutions. The migration from rural areas contributes to the problems of both the city and the countryside, by depopulating rural places at the expense of overcrowded cities. Solutions to rural problems consequently will benefit both rural and urban people and will give America a new lease on life.

This book, *The Development of Rural America*, is about rural-development processes, problems, and solutions. It should provide valuable guidelines for policies to benefit both rural and urban areas. Although the title contains the word "rural," the content of the book focuses on the development of both (a) the open country and small towns, and (b) smaller cities (up to fifty thousand population). The book consists of seven papers written as original contributions by prominent agricultural and regional economists, demographers, and administrators. The book also has been carefully edited to provide continuity throughout. It is prepared in three parts:

Part 1: The Nature of Rural Development (2 papers)

Part 2: The Social and Economic Condition of Rural America (2 papers)

Part 3: Rural Development Alternatives (3 papers)

Part 1 is designed to provide an understanding of the general nature of rural development. The two papers in this section focus on the community and area (multicounty) aspects of rural development. These two approaches are largely overlapping rather than mutually exclusive, and both area and community efforts may be integrated with individual actions to provide effective development. The first paper, "The Philosophy and Process of Community Development," is written by J. Carroll Bottum, Hillenbrand Distinguished Professor of Agricultural Economics at Purdue University and lifelong practitioner of community development. This paper examines community development as a group decision-making process and looks at the organization of citizens committees for community development. The second paper in Part 1, "The Emergence of Area Development," written by Richard Hausler, examines the evolution and characteristics of present and proposed development programs. Richard Hausler has served as administrator to several federal area-development and antipoverty agencies, and was executive director of the National Area Development Institute at Lexington, Kentucky, at the time his paper was written.

Part 2 provides a summary of the social and economic conditions of small cities, towns, and the open country throughout America. This section begins with "Trends in the U.S. Rural Population," written by Calvin Beale, rural population specialist of the Department of Agriculture. This paper analyzes current 1970 census data to summarize recent patterns of rural population growth and decline, migration, and the effects of population change. The fourth paper "The Condition and Problems of Nonmetropolitan America," by George Brinkman, formerly of Kansas State University and now Associate Professor of Agricultural Economics at the University of Guelph (Ontario, Canada), examines rural employment and income opportunities in agricultural and nonagricultural jobs, and summarizes the relatively poor condition of rural health care, education, and housing.

Part 3 examines some rural-development alternatives, including national development programs, the development and use of natural resources, and policies for dealing with rural poverty. "Systems Planning for Rural Development" is the first paper in this section. It is written by Luther Tweeten, Regents Distinguished Professor of Agricultural Economics at Oklahoma State University. This paper presents a framework for national planning on the basis of the cost effectiveness of programs, and analyzes the effectiveness of many of the federal government's programs. Emery N. Castle, Dean of the Graduate School and former chairman of the department of agricultural economics at Oregon State University, is the author of the sixth paper, "Natural Resource Use in Community Development." This paper examines some implications of developing natural resources on the options that communities may use for their individual development and on the distribution of income through resource-development projects.

The final paper is "Rural Poverty and Urban Growth: An Economic Critique of Alternative Spatial Growth Patterns," by Niles M. Hansen, Director of the Center for Economic Development and prominent regional economist at the University of Texas. This paper analyzes the problem of rural poverty and relates its solution to investments in growth centers and intermediate-sized cities (250,000 population) rather than investments in infrastructure in lagging rural areas. Niles Hansen also recommends greater investment in human-resource development through education and training, so that residents of lagging areas will be able to migrate more successfully to intermediate centers for jobs and better living conditions. Since Hansen's recommendations are oriented toward moving people out of rural areas rather than promoting development within these areas, his proposals are controversial. It is hoped that this paper will lead to greater interest in finding effective solutions to rural poverty.

These papers have been carefully selected and edited to provide an integrated approach to rural development, rather than just a series of readings. The material on developmental processes, rural conditions and problems, and development alternatives should be beneficial reading to serious students of rural development and to interested laymen alike.

George L. Brinkman

Contents

1

The Nature
of Rural
Development

THE PHILOSOPHY
AND PROCESS OF
COMMUNITY DEVELOPMENT

J. CARROLL BOTTUM / Purdue University

Every time we make a significant technological advance, we create the necessity for economic, social, environmental, or institutional changes in our community. Thus, rapid changes in these areas are necessary in periods of rapid technological change. The thought has been expressed by many people in recent years that we are in a technical and social revolution and that we are closer to its beginning than we are to its end. If this is true, and there is good reason to believe that it is, the task of developing and redeveloping the human environment and the human community is among the most important concerns of our society.

Nearly every citizen, from one in the smallest hamlet to the resident of one of our great metropolises or from the individual voter to a member of Congress, supports the concept of community improvement in its broadest sense. It is when we talk about how it is to be brought about and what kind of development we want that sparks begin to fly. This paper is designed to clarify the philosophy and process of community development in rural areas. It also looks at some difficulties with regard to community development that arise because of requiring decisions from groups as well as from specialized public agencies. Finally, this paper examines the approach to community development in Indiana through citizens'

3

committees, to provide an example of organization and development procedures that have been successful there.

COMMUNITY DEVELOPMENT DEFINED

When we talk about community development, it is first necessary for us to have an understanding of the terms "community" and "community development." A community is usually defined as a group of people who organize for a common purpose, and in this sense an individual can belong to many communities. He may belong to one community in connection with the primary school for his children, to another from the standpoint of taxes, to another where he trades, to another from the standpoint of his cultural center, and so on. Thus, a community may be large or small in geographic area depending upon the function involved. It may also consist of many different types of people, such as businessmen, farmers, housewives, children, retired people, servicemen, school teachers, and many others.

The term "community development" is defined differently by many people. This is natural at this stage of community development. However, if we are to make the most progress, we need to agree basically on what activity we are discussing, even though we may use slightly different terms to describe it. I should like to define community development as an effort to increase the economic opportunity and the quality of living of a given community through helping the people of that community with those problems that require group decision and group action.

The terms "economic opportunity" and "quality of living" are as broad in scope and in subject matter as anyone could desire. They include developing new jobs; providing better services; construction of homes, streets, and sewers; developing good school systems; providing opportunities for the elderly; recreation; and a host of other activities. The phrase "with those problems that require group decision and group action" is restrictive in the sense that it rules out all problems that may be solved on an individual basis. For example, under this definition, whether a county should have an educational program in the wise use of credit might be a community-resource-development issue, but the providing of an individual family with information for making a credit decision would not be a community-resource-development activity.

Some might define community development as making the community a better place in which to work and to live. This puts every activity of the Extension Service and nearly every other community organization under the umbrella of community development. It is an appealing approach but not very useful in developing programs. It is not sufficiently definitive to be workable as an activity. Community development needs to zero in on the group decisions of the community and not dissipate its energies on everything.

Some might also argue that this definition does not allow for measurement of progress. It is granted that it is difficult to measure progress when the criteria for each community are different. However, it is unrealistic to assume that there is a set of criteria that fits all communities. There simply is not such a set of criteria. The people of a given community can tell you whether the community-development work in their community helped them to reach their goals. Quality of life is like beauty—it is in the eye of the beholder.

Community-resource development is an effort to combine the body of known knowledge in the area of community development with the brainpower of the community for the purpose of speeding up and improving the solving of community problems. A basic premise in community development is that only the people of a community may determine what should be its goals after they have been made aware of the problems and opportunities of their particular community. The value judgments are rendered by community leaders, not by the technicians who carry out the development projects or by educators who may be helping the community in its decision-making. The technicians should be on tap but not on top.

The Community-Development Process

Community development may be involved only in helping communities effectively carry out whatever activities certain groups are sponsoring or may decide to sponsor, or it may be involved in the broader context of determining what the goals of the community should be, what the fundamental problems are, and what the priorities in the problems attacked in the community should be. To my way of thinking, if community development is to progress and move ahead on a sound basis, it must eventually take this last approach.

Many groups are ready to champion a cause. The real gap in our communities is the making of an analysis of the community's

5

problems and opportunities, the crystallizing of opinion based on sound analysis, the setting of priorities, and the developing of workable alternatives as a basis for communities to make rational decisions. Successful corporations have divisions to analyze and set forth alternative opportunities for their boards of directors. Successful communities require so much technical information and are affected so much by trends and developments that they need some way to combine technicians with the influence leaders, to do the same thing that happens in well-run corporations.

The community-development process is a decision-making process. This process is outlined in figure 1 and begins with people who are concerned about their community. These concerned individuals must collect, analyze, and interpret background information about their community to properly identify the problems that they are confronted with. Also, if the community is going to find lasting solutions, they must determine their goals and the kind of development they desire. Since many problems may be present, the most important should be identified as priority areas. Furthermore, each problem may have several possible alternative solutions with different consequences of each. Each solution must be examined to see if it is feasible and how it should be carried out. These possible

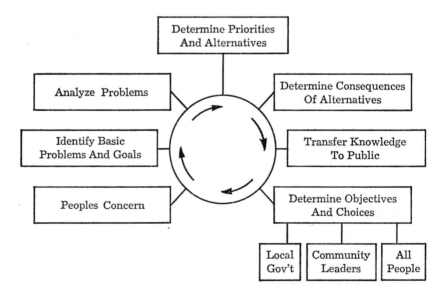

FIGURE 1   THE COMMUNITY-DEVELOPMENT PROCESS

6

alternative solutions, consequences, and strategies for action need to be made known to the whole community, so that the various groups and individuals of the community can properly choose objectives and solutions. These choices may be made by many different organizations and groups, ranging from local government units and community leaders to all of the people in the community.

When this decision-making process has been properly carried out, the implementation of the development programs becomes a technical procedure, which is not included in the community-development process. For example, the decision to have a youth-training program and how to implement it might well be community development, but once such a program was under way it would not be considered community development. This would be true even though the activity might be contributing greatly to the economic opportunity of the community. If an architect becomes involved in the actual construction of all the houses he plans, he soon becomes diverted from his real task. This does not mean that he does not study how the houses he designs meet his clients' desires in the final analysis.

The educator's role in community development involves helping a community to identify and define its goals broadly. He helps the community identify and rate the importance of various problems in attaining its goals. He helps the community put the problem in a decision-making framework. He develops new alternatives for the community by inventing new arrangements or institutions to take care of new situations. He helps the community measure the cost and benefits of each alternative. He helps the community in its strategy in carrying out its objectives after it chooses the approach it wishes to use. But he leaves the actual decision-making up to the community.

Leadership and Community Structure

If community-development workers are going to contribute most effectively to better decisions, they must have access to the decision-makers. In some way the decision-makers must be found and exposed to useful information, just as the decision-makers in a business must be involved if technology is to be changed.

Not everyone becomes involved in the community-development process. Leadership and participation will vary greatly between communities. Generally, however, the structure of the community can be stratified among leaders, followers, and nonparticipants, as shown in figure 2. At the top of the pyramid is a small group of influence leaders, followed by a larger group of action-oriented people. Beneath these two leadership groups are found larger groups of interested citizens and also those who do not care. Often the group of people who do not care is the largest group within the community.

The influence leaders are the people in the community with foresight and awareness who are able to identify the community-development problems and their solutions. They have become influence leaders in the community because of their record in past decisions of being correct and timely. This group is looked on by the rest of the citizens as a source of information and ideas and decision-making expertise. They usually are the best qualified to serve on a community-development committee.

The second group of leaders in the community are the action-oriented people. This group is somewhat larger than that of the influence leaders, and it often includes the leaders of civic organizations and action groups. Its members are looked on by the community as the people who can get things done, but they may not necessarily be asked for the initial decisions and ideas. Both the influence leaders and the action-oriented leadership group are important in community development. The responsibility for community-development decisions will rest primarily with the influence leaders, while the action-oriented leadership group will usually have the responsibility for implementing these decisions.

FIGURE 2   COMMUNITY-PARTICIPATION TRIANGLE

The charge is made by some reformers that working with the influence leaders tends to perpetuate the status quo. Working with this group does not decrease the opportunity for the crusaders to work in the community. As the attitudes of the community change, the influence leaders change. By being sensitive to the community's attitudes was the very way they became influential. The very fact that these individuals are willing to get together and study the potentialities of their communities insures a certain amount of open-mindedness.

Some community professionals get the idea that the influence leaders shape the community and that, therefore, all groups should be represented on the committee to see that their rights are protected. The influence leaders have influence because they do represent the attitudes and goals of the total community and are experts at timing and putting operating legs on community programs. The people in any community who have this ability are scarce. If you bring together representatives of various pressure groups, you are right back in the political arena again; and we already have our political system for making decisions of this type. Major decisions worked on by a community-development committee are still settled by the political process, but they may be decided differently because of the better understanding and better proposals that may be brought to the public by the community-development committee.

Community-development efforts must take into consideration the special characteristics of each community. These characteristics can be grouped into four different systems:

1. The political system
2. The cultural system
3. The social system
4. The economic and technical system

Each of these systems contributes to the way people act, think, and work within the community. Differences in these systems between communities account for major differences in the approaches and results of community development. Each community, for example, may have a different political system and may vary in the extent of participation by its citizens, the attitudes of the power structure in the community, and the receptivity of elected officials to suggestions for needed changes. Cultural influences may also influence community decisions. Entertainment that includes the serving of alcoholic beverages is certainly accepted differently among the German immigrants of Wisconsin and among many of the citizens of Kansas. Social systems may influence where people live in the community, and they may be important in determining which programs will be acceptable. Likewise, the economic and technical system within the community may determine which programs are feasible, such as the kinds of employment opportunities that can be developed in the community. These four systems are important determinants of how community members will react to community changes. They are the structure within which community development must take place.

INNOVATIONS AND COMMUNITY DECISION-MAKING

We are making progress in community development, but this progress has come slowly and with much hard work. One of the reasons for the relative slowness of this progress is the nature of community change.

Community development is a group decision process. Most of our business and personal decisions, however, are individual ones. In the last one hundred years we have made great technical advances in agriculture. Each individual farmer or manager has had an opportunity to take this technical information by himself, evaluate it, and either adopt or reject it. These were individual choices. When it comes to community changes, however, over 50 percent of the group involved must make up their minds the same way at the same time. Thus, it is much more difficult for a community to arrive at decisions and to take action than it is for a single individual.

A good example of differences in individual and group adoption of technological change is the introduction of tractors. As a boy, I went to the first tractor plowing demonstration in our rural community. There were two tractors: the old Titan and another make, which I cannot remember. The demonstrators showed how rapidly they could plow. A group of our neighbors went in a lumber wagon. On the way home they appraised the tractors and everyone agreed that he would not have one because it would pack the ground, it would break down, it was too costly, and so on. The group decision on tractor adoption here was negative. But do you know, there was one crazy farmer who bought one (he didn't have the approval of the American Horse Association either). This model ran only part of the time, but with a little work it was improved. One by one we bought tractors and mechanized American agriculture. So it has been with adoption of other technologies, with a few individuals accepting the change where the group as a whole would not. If group choice had been required for the adoption of all our technologies, we might still be plowing with horses today.

In addition to slowing the adoption of technical improvements, group decision-making also has impaired rapid adjustment in our social institutions. Today many communities are faced with a great need to renovate and improve many of their social institutions that changing technology and social values have rendered obsolete. Slower response through group decisions than by individual action has often caused a great lag in the adjustment of these institutions and at times has made community progress toward improvement of them difficult.

CITIZENS COMMITTEES FOR COMMUNITY DEVELOPMENT

If community services and development are going to be relevant and coordinated with the people of the community, they must be related to them through some form of a citizens' committee or committees. Processes must be developed so that communities, whether they be on a basis of growth centers, counties, or smaller areas, exercise more power of coordination and direction.

In my observation and study, there is no substitute for the part that citizens' committees play in community development, whether in the rural or urban areas, in this country or abroad. This is true no matter how many official boards, agencies, or planning groups are established.

Members of action organizations and agencies often say that community-development study groups only get involved in lengthy discussions, whereas their organizations are the ones that finance the housing or get the sewers and water lines laid—the things that really count in community development. Of course, both types of organizations are needed; for improvements such as housing or sewer and water lines may actually compound the problems of the community if the total needs of the community and the implications for the community are not taken into consideration. This sometimes happens, just as some community-development groups do nothing but talk. Nevertheless, saying that a community does not need an effective overall development group is like saying that in order to

11

construct buildings it is only necessary to have masons, carpenters, plumbers, and painters, that it is not necessary to have any input from owners, architects, or contractors.

In every community, decisions are being made every day. There are people in every community who are making decisions for that community or choosing not to make decisions, regardless of whether we have a community program going on or not, or whether we think highly of the quality of the decisions being made. This is an obvious observation, but often we tend to forget it. The function of community-development activity is to tie into this operation and to coordinate, speed up, and improve the quality of the decisions being made.

If better coordination of the community goals and services is to be obtained, the citizens of influence or the natural leaders must be brought together for the same vigorous study and analysis that they use in their businesses and professions. They likewise must be serviced by the best knowledge that is available concerning community management.

Furthermore, experience would indicate that from lists of these leaders an overall committee of 75 to 150 should be selected. This committee would only meet once to four times per year and would have the responsibility of determining the community problems and setting priorities. A smaller committee would be involved in making studies and recommendations to the larger committee and in trying to get the suggested action.

These larger committees should also include representatives from all government agencies located in the county who are involved in action programs for community improvement. This is important in getting greater coordination at the local level. Today each agency has good interagency communication from the local level to the state or national level. However, many of the local problems require a coordinated approach of several agencies. This coordination between agencies at both the state and national level leaves much to be desired.

In Indiana, we have used an approach for selecting citizens' committees by interviewing a group of forty to fifty active leaders who are interested in various community activities. These leaders are asked to name, say, five people that they believe are dedicated, broad-minded, highly respected individuals, sensitive to the community's needs, whom they would like to see entrusted with developing the community. On this assembled list will appear individuals who have been named several times. The thirty to forty people named most often by this group are next interviewed and asked the same questions. From both of these lists the fifteen to twenty-five individuals most often named are then taken as a community committee. The second list generally tends to center on certain individuals more than the first list, and the silent leaders come into greater prominence.

In the rural communities, where the background and goals of the people are more homogeneous, one tends to get an influence group that fairly well represents, as a group, the total community. In the more complex industrial communities, one gets a merging of leaders, each of whom may represent the background and goals of individual groups in the community. This makes more complex the problem of operating a community-development program. It requires modifications in some of the approaches used, as compared to rural communities. The greater use of mass media becomes more necessary in the larger, more complex communities.

In every one of our communities, there are many official and nonofficial groups organized to study and carry out programs. We believe the uniqueness and strength of community-development committees rests on their not having any official power and not becoming directly active in any particular cause. These people are the thinkers and planners, not the ones to carry out the programs. Their skills are too scarce and heavily committed to allow them to become involved in the action phase of development. The members' satisfactions must come from helping the community realistically think through its problems in an integrated manner, in helping to establish community goals, in inventing new approaches, in encouraging education when needed, in determining priorities and timing, and, finally, from seeing things happen in the community in which they know they had a part. This is the way such people have always achieved their satisfaction. The job of carrying out the programs then falls on the already established or newly established official and nonofficial action organizations. These organizations also receive the credit or blame.

There are at least two requirements for the success of such committees: (1) They must not be responsible to any action organization, and (2) they must not become involved in action as a committee.

I have seen such committees successfully organized by Cooperative Extension, the Chamber of Commerce, lawyers, bankers, and others. But the ones that were successful over a period of time had to abide by the previously mentioned restraints. They also had to be served by some unusual individual or some organization.

In Indiana, we have thirty such committees operating. They vary from a county like Parke, with 15,000 people, to a county like Lake, with 600,000 people. Lake County includes such cities as East Chicago, Hammond, and Gary. The committees in Parke have been operating for fifteen years; the one in Lake, for four years. Such committees usually meet regularly once a month. They are working on problems from human relations to parks, governmental reorganization, and solid-waste disposal. The most important thing is that they are working on problems that are important to the people of their communities.

THE EMERGENCE
OF AREA
DEVELOPMENT

RICHARD HAUSLER / National Area Development Institute

In recent years, many new decision-making processes and organizations have been developed to provide a better distribution of our population and better development of our country. These decision-making processes and organizations have emerged at many levels of government—from federal and state levels to multicounty districts and local communities—to provide a new approach for the development of metropolitan and nonmetropolitan areas alike. These efforts will be referred to as area development, because they are designed to provide assistance simultaneously to many communities and geographic areas. In contrast, the term community development refers primarily to the development efforts of individual communities. Area-development efforts are designed to provide assistance to larger geographic areas to tackle many of the problems that are too large for single communities.

Area development, like community development, can be defined in various ways. Certainly, descriptions of area development must include the elements of community development, as both are designed to enable citizens to use effectively all available resources in order to set and attain their economic, social, and political goals. However, since area development generally involves several towns as well as counties in a common effort to improve the quality of

15

life throughout the entire area, increased coordination is needed among governmental levels, geographic areas, and specialized services. Area development represents a new kind of federalism, through which technicians, private citizens, and government officials attempt to coordinate their efforts for local, multicounty, state, and federal development. Area development, therefore, may be described as community development on a large scale.

This paper is divided into two sections. The evolution of area-development decision-making processes and organizations during the past decade is the topic of the first section. The second section examines new laws and current proposals under consideration in Congress today; it also outlines some of the problems to be faced in future efforts. Both sections will concentrate on nonmetropolitan areas. These areas represent rural places, towns, and smaller cities that have not yet encountered population congestion, oversaturation, and other problems of the huge strip cities.

THE EVOLUTION OF AREA-DEVELOPMENT PROGRAMS

The new area-development decision-making processes and organizations created in the past decade were designed to reorganize governmental efforts and to assist in directing the investment of public and private capital. These processes and organizations were established by federal, state, and local action as a result of national recognition of several facts:

1. It became apparent that certain parts of the country—in some cases, a few counties and, in others, whole regions, like Appalachia or the old Cotton Belt of the South—were lagging even in period of rapid national economic growth.

2. It became apparent that in all regions there were many people—perhaps 35 million in the mid 1960s—who were living in poverty amid growing affluence.

3. Problems began emerging because so many of our people were piling up in major metropolitan centers at a rate that, if continued, would result in some 77 percent of 300 million people living in twenty-two cities by the year 2000.

4. In recent years, more people—particularly the young in this era of big universities, big government, and big businesses—began demonstrating a desire to have more voice in the decisions affecting their lives, to attain some individuality.

16

Recognizing these problems, federal, state, and local governments began organizing and developing new programs to improve rural and urban living conditions. These programs were designed to (1) foster economic development of depressed areas or regions; (2) eradicate poverty and improve health, education, and welfare of our citizens; (3) attain better distribution of our population through better-balanced rural-urban growth; and (4) give citizens a bigger voice in decisions that affect their lives.

The evolution of programs by which action was taken to get at stagnation, poverty, population imbalance, and the loss of individual decisions is particularly important, as these programs represent the development of political and administrative thinking about how these problems should be solved. First, let us look at the federal programs. The pieces of legislation included here and the names of agencies involved are not as important as the kind of programs and the administrative procedures that they represent.

Federal Programs

First, there was an attempt to get at area stagnation—the depressed areas. The Area Redevelopment Act in 1961 became the first major piece of President Kennedy's program to be enacted. The law provided for infusion of capital into areas of low income and high unemployment by (1) soft, low-interest public loans to encourage private investments in industrial and business expansion in these depressed areas, and (2) loans and grants to depressed communities to finance the water, sewage, and other facilities needed to support industrial facilities.

In addition to this public investment of capital to stimulate private investment in these depressed areas, the Area Redevelopment Act started something else which, little noticed, has been built into numerous other programs. Responsibilities for determining how to spend public dollars and for setting community or area priorities were put in the hands of area organizations controlled by public officials *and* representatives of private groups in the area: business, labor, agriculture, and the like.

In 1964 the Economic Opportunity Act was passed to get at the poverty persisting amid affluence in all areas. The Office of Economic Opportunity (OEO) was established, with funds for a whole host of activities designed to help the poor. Without going into its

17

merits and the weaknesses of individual OEO programs, some relevant points should be noted.

First, *community action organizations* were sponsored, with funds made available to staff them. Here again, we have the creation of public-private bodies to make decisions regarding the spending of public money. These organizations were required by law to have boards on which the program's beneficiaries—the poor, by whatever euphemism—serve. By regulation, the poor were to supply one-third of the board members, while public officials were to occupy one-third of the seats and other citizens the remaining one-third.

As the area-redevelopment and antipoverty organizations began to function, it became apparent that in most cases the individual nonmetropolitan county or town was an inadequate base for any significant economic-development or antipoverty program. Consequently, development of larger area units was encouraged. At OEO in the days of its conception and infancy, federal dollars were used to encourage the formation of multicounty community-action organizations to make possible the programs of sufficient scope and size as required by law. Priority was simply given to those groups that would work together across county lines. Thus emerged multijurisdictional community-action agencies.

Then, in 1965, legislation was passed establishing the Appalachian Regional Commission. Here again, there was a built-in incentive (through funds for staffing and other means) to encourage the formation of multicounty public-private organizations to set area goals and to establish priorities for the spending of public dollars to develop areas.

But the legislation went beyond this: it set up the Appalachian Regional Commission as a device to encourage federal-state cooperation. The Commission is headed by a federal cochairman and a states' cochairman. The federal cochairman is appointed, while the states' cochairman is elected by and from the thirteen Appalachian governors. A staff, headed by the representative of the states, does staff work for the governors.

In 1965, also, the Economic Development Act became law. As noted, this superseded the Area Redevelopment Act. It included incentive for the establishment of multicounty economic development districts, provided funds to staff such organizations, and required

18

public and private representation on controlling boards. This act also enabled creation of regional commissions—pale versions of the Appalachian Regional Commission—for lagging regions of the country: New England, the old Cotton Belt along southeastern coasts, the Upper Great Lakes Region, the Ozarks, and a region made up of large portions of Utah, Arizona, Colorado, and New Mexico.

These programs are representative of still a number of other national programs built on multicounty organizations, federal-state coordination, and public and private involvement in controlling investments, which will not be examined here. Suffice it to say that such programs and such structures have resulted in the establishment of comprehensive health councils, regional crime councils, districts for resource conservation and development, organizations for control of air pollution and water pollution, model-cities agencies, HUD-funded planning districts, and others.

Without going into more detail on this host of laws and programs, let us summarize some of the themes that run through them:

1. Multicounty organizations are encouraged or required.
2. A voice by private citizens, the beneficiaries of the different programs, is required or encouraged. The programs are designed so that the poor have a voice in antipoverty programs, that labor has a voice in economic-development programs, and that users as well as doctors have a voice in comprehensive health programs.
3. Coordination of federal, state, and local public investments with private investment is required or encouraged.
4. A role for state government is provided, both through veto powers and through staffs for state governors funded largely by federal dollars.

This whole trend of development programs has been supported by technical assistance by thousands of federal employees in the Departments of Commerce, Agriculture, Labor, HUD, HEW, and from independent agencies such as the Small Business Administration and OEO. Furthermore, preference has been given in numerous federal loan and grant programs to projects blessed by area and regional organizations.

State-Federal Area-Development Efforts

The discussion thus far has been concerned primarily with the federal role in development. Concurrently a number of states had been moving in the same direction, often coordinating their development efforts with federal programs. As early as the late 1950s, Georgia passed legislation to set up multicounty planning and development districts. Through legislation and gubernatorial executive orders, other states have established their own programs and substate districts to implement them. These districts generally are drawn up to include several counties with similar agriculture, business opportunities, development problems, and so forth, usually with some growth center in the area.

The federal government has encouraged states to establish such multijurisdictional development organizations. In addition to making funds available to governors to establish clearing houses and give technical assistance, administrative procedures have been altered to encourage these organizational trends. More recently, with the support of some of the programs mentioned earlier and planning grants from the Department of Housing and Urban Development, state governments have also assumed a larger role in setting development priorities. Statewide planning and state assistance to area organizations in drawing up their own plans are being handled in several states through a staff responsible to the governor. In some states, notably Texas and Georgia, state budgets are drawn up on the basis of these plans.

It is in these multijurisdictional area organizations that the public-private organizations must make investment decisions. This is true of most of the multijurisdictional planning and development agencies. Typically these organizations are controlled by a board composed of 51 percent or more public officials, with the remainder being private citizens representing different segments of the community: business, labor, agriculture, education, health, and the like. These boards, which generally are assisted by a staff and technicians from the state and federal governments, set goals for the area and list priority projects. Among them they must work out the tradeoffs, considering what federal and state money is available and what the cost to the area will be.

State and federal governments do not automatically approve the investments in priority projects set by these area boards; but those decisions are given great weight in most cases and are often determinate.

Some Problems and Progress

Capital investments are necessary in the development of an area or region. Despite the billions of dollars of federal, state, and local tax money in public development programs, however, it appears to be nearly impossible to bring about the desired changes by public capital alone, at least without completely altering our form of government. Most public development programs, therefore, are attempting to provide mechanisms through which government at all levels can trigger the necessary private investments to sustain area development.

The decision-making process in area development is new and imperfect. Some of the area organizations obviously make their decisions primarily on the basis of how much state and federal money is available for certain kinds of projects. Boards are generally inexperienced. Sometimes their staffs are headed by politicians who did not do too well in the last election or local businessmen who happen to be available. Sometimes the boards are dominated by one segment of the community or another.

We know, too, that this whole process and the public programs supporting it have not yet triggered the necessary private investments. Town bankers, for example, generally continute to invest a smaller part of their funds in local enterprises than city banks do. As a result, there is a net outflow of capital from nonmetropolitan areas, which need it most.

This is a human problem. Presidents of many of these banks are in their sixties or older. Shaken by the depression in their youth, seeking security rather than venture, accustomed more to dealing with agriculture than industry, they are often more inclined to invest in treasury bills than in the business dreams of a local young man.

There is also the old farm antipathy toward industrial and business development, particularly in agricultural states. Much of this antipathy goes back to old fears that growth would mean competition for labor, thus driving up the cost of hired hands. This factor is no longer important in most areas, because little farm labor is hired; but many farm leaders, like many bank presidents, are older men, so old ideas prevail. Frequently, therefore, you have the local farm organization in direct opposition to labor and the Chamber of Commerce.

Furthermore, considerable confusion exists in governmental units as state and local governments, organized in another day, attempt to face problems of the last third of the twentieth century. Overlaps, conflicts, and duplication result as these institutions lumberingly try to adapt old agencies to the new problems.

Despite these handicaps, this process called area development is getting established across the country. As imperfect as it is, it must be judged on the basis of the question, "Compared to what?"

Compared to old approaches which got us into this population imbalance mess we are in?

Compared to development decisions made in Washington for every area in the country?

Compared to every small town and every nonmetropolitan county trying to go it alone?

Compared to each segment of each community—health, education, industrial development—going it alone as if its decisions do not have impacts on other segments?

Compared to decision-making processes in which one group or another is in the saddle to the exclusion of other groups and individuals?

Progress is being made in the development of nonmetropolitan areas. It is true that the population of nonmetropolitan areas grew by only 7 percent during the sixties, while metropolitan areas grew by 16.4 percent, for a national growth of 13 percent. The overall growth in nonmetropolitan areas, however, is low, because it includes a 36 percent drop in the farm population—a drop of some 5 million people. Substantial increases were shown by the nonfarm, nonmetropolitan population, along with progress in nonmetropolitan area development, as indicated by the following figures.

1. The nonfarm, nonmetropolitan population of the nation increased 19.2 percent during the decade, exceeding the rate of metropolitan increase by almost 3 percent.

2. Despite the drastic drop in farm population, the net outmigration from nonmetropolitan areas in the sixties fell to 2.5 million from the 5 million of the fifties.

3. Nonmetropolitan, nonfarm jobs increased by 37.5 percent from 1962 to 1968, compared with a 23.6 percent increase in the urban areas.

It is apparent that if these trends continue at their present rate, now that drops in farm population can no longer be so drastic, the rate of nonmetropolitan population growth will accelerate considerably in the 1970s.

To those who have been following rural industrialization, these figures are not surprising. Statistics on industrial employment in the mid sixties began showing a trend toward towns and rural areas. In 1968 a meeting sponsored by the federal government with top officials of fifty-six major manufacturing companies indicated that, with one exception, they were planning to locate most of their branch plants near small cities or towns. (The exception was a company that wanted to avoid the community responsibilities a big company must assume in a small town.)

The census figures do show dramatic reversals in some of the depressed areas that have attracted so much developmental attention in the past decade. There is, for example, a large area in southeastern Oklahoma, northeastern Texas, and southwestern Arkansas where a decline has been replaced by rather rapid growth. Some Appalachian areas in eastern Tennessee, western North Carolina, and western Kentucky have reversed trends dramatically. Subjectively, much of the development in these areas can be traced to a few individuals who made effective use of all the federal and state development tools available to them.

Furthermore, the successful development efforts have concentrated on comprehensive improvement of a great many community facilities and services, not just one or two. A community or area, for example, is probably wasting its time if it just goes smokestack-chasing while it neglects its total environment—its schools, health facilities, housing, recreation, and its air and water. Except for tramp industries that milk one community for all possible concessions and then move on, industries today are concerned about the total environment of the community in which they locate. After all, their employees read the papers and have kids, like the rest of us. They must attract employees who also are concerned about a decent community for their familes.

NEW PROPOSALS FOR AREA DEVELOPMENT (AS OF 1971)

Several relevant proposals to improve and accelerate area development are currently under discussion and consideration in Congress. One of these programs supported by a number of different people in Congress and in the administration, which has implications for a great many other programs, is the development of a national-growth policy.

National Policy for Population Distribution

The establishment of a national-growth policy is supported by both the president and a number of key congressmen. This policy would consist of a deliberate effort by the government to direct economic activity and the location of population growth. Such a policy would then be instrumental in affecting all kinds of other decisions, such as where to locate highways, governmental services, defense contracts, and other industrial-development incentives. This policy, for example, could be utilized to encourage the development of nonmetropolitan areas and to discourage further growth of the huge metropolitan areas.

The Family Assistance Plan

Another proposal which could have a decisive effect on population distribution is the Family Assistance Plan that is being advocated by President Nixon. In some states in the Deep South in which there are large numbers of poorly educated and unemployed people, the levels of assistance are very low. The proposed Family Assistance Plan would provide for much more uniform levels of assistance nationally, so that families in the South would no longer need to move to New York or Chicago to receive enough assistance to live on. The pressures to migrate to the major cities would be further reduced by including the HEW proposals to provide training with the Family Assistance Plan, whereby participants could become employed in the states in which they reside.

Industrial Incentives for Rural Location

Several pieces of legislation have also been drawn up to encourage location of industry in rural areas. These programs are generally of two types. An example of the first type is the Rural Job Development Act introduced by Senators Pearson and Harris to give tax incentives to industries that locate in rural areas. These programs are designed to induce the large viable corporations, such as General Motors, General Electric, IBM, and so on, who have little trouble in securing financing and loans, to move in the direction of rural areas. The second type of program is designed to provide subsidized financing, loan guarantees, and/or long-term loans for non-blue-chip companies which may have difficulty in obtaining the necessary financing for operation. Many industries in rural areas fall into this category, as most of the banks in the smaller cities and towns do not like to make loans for longer than five years and consider rural industries as risky endeavors.

Programs to Increase Private Capital

Two types of programs are also under consideration to increase the amount of private capital in rural areas. The first type of program is designed to establish public lending agencies. A second bill introduced by Senator Pearson, the Rural Community Development Bank Act, would have the federal government establish and provide seed money for a banking system that would get private financing into rural job-development enterprises. Other proposals are designed to set up a development bank but not limit this bank to nonmetropolitan areas. Still another proposal would get the farm-credit system into nonfarm lending.

The second type of program is designed to direct the use of public funds deposited in private banks. In this program, governmental agencies agree to deposit surplus or reserve public funds in private banks, provided that these banks agree to invest a certain percentage of this amount in development projects. This type of program is now utilized by some federal development agencies. They encourage recipients of their aid to put their funds for development in private banks only under the stipulation that the banks utilize these funds for further development, rather than for purchasing treasury bills or for making other investments that do not contribute to the development of that district.

Revenue-Sharing

Perhaps the most controversial proposal is the issue of revenue-sharing. There are two parts of the president's 1970 revenue-sharing package. One would provide $5 billion in grants to states, with no earmarking for special purposes. The second part of the revenue-sharing package would provide some $11 billion in grants for a half-dozen general types of expenditures, with $1.1 billion of that for rural development. Each state would draw up a development plan to spend this money to develop its rural areas. Rural areas are defined as those that have a population density of fewer than one hundred persons per square mile or are outside a Standard Metropolitan Statistical Area.

There is quite a bit of controversy swirling about this proposal, because most of the $1.1 billion for rural development would come as a result of national termination of several federal programs presently affecting rural development. The Appalachian Regional Commission, Economic Development Administration grants, Farmers Home Administration grants for water and waste disposal, and federal support of the Cooperative Extension Service all would be terminated, with the funds previously used for these programs lumped together to be used by each state as it sees fit. This means that each state would have to decide whether it wants to continue a state version of these programs or use the shared revenue for other rural-development purposes.

The passage of revenue-sharing in this form appears unlikely. By early 1971 the Senate had already approved by a 77 to 3 vote the extension of the Appalachian and EDA programs, which the President was counting on for almost half of the revenue for rural development. The present revenue-sharing proposal has also run into opposition in the House of Representatives from Representative Wilbur Mills, the powerful chairman of the Ways and Means Committee. Continuation of the Appalachian and EDA programs has also been pushed by Representative John Blatnik, who wants to add an accelerated public-works program. The latter would provide loans and grants for public facilities to meet community development needs and stimulate the economy.

Even though revenue-sharing in its present form is unlikely to be passed at this time, sufficient pressures at state and national levels are present to continue or increase support for revenue-sharing and increased federal spending for rural development. The present proposal and any future proposals that would require a reorganization of governmental agencies, however, are likely to run into many difficulties in implementation at the local level in the near future.

Although multicounty units and multidisciplinary approaches have been emphasized in recent development programs, very few states are well enough organized at this point in time to utilize this approach. Most efforts for development of nonmetropolitan areas are still being undertaken by special-purpose agencies, often operating within a single county or community and uncoordinated with other development efforts. While the new revenue-sharing proposal offers an opportunity to reorganize development efforts on a multicounty basis and a multidisciplinary approach (at the expense of existing programs), few states have multicounty districts that are staffed, operationalized, and capable of utilizing federal funds on a multicounty basis. There is no administrative structure in most states to handle a large influx of funds, such the revenue-sharing proposal would provide, without being forced to channel these funds through the existing special-purpose administrative structures. Consequently this new revenue-sharing proposal, while providing an opportunity for a new, integrated area-wide rural-development effort, unfortunately may be somewhat premature, as the administrative structure in most states is insufficiently developed on a multicounty basis to take advantage of this new opportunity.

These new programs are some of the most important ones currently under consideration in Congress. It is always difficult to predict what will happen in national legislation, but support for rural development is present from both parties in Congress. It does seem certain that more national emphasis will be given to rural-community development in the future than at any time in the past.

EDITOR'S UPDATING ON REVENUE-SHARING

In 1972 Congress passed a new revenue-sharing law providing federal funds to governmental units throughout the United States over a five-year period. The new law differs from the president's original proposal in 1970 in several ways. First, the new law does not earmark funds for any specific purposes, such as rural development, so that communities may allocate all the funds themselves. Second, it utilizes only new, additional funds rather than redistributing funds from existing agencies. Finally, the new law authorizes greater appropriations. Over the five-year period it will provide $30.2 billion in indirect financial assistance to cities, counties, and states as follows:

1 Jan.–30 June 1972 .... $ 2.650 billion
1 July–31 Dec. 1972 .... $ 2.650 billion

1 Jan.–30 June 1973	$ 2.987 billion
Fiscal Year 1974	$ 6.050 billion
Fiscal Year 1975	$ 6.200 billion
Fiscal Year 1976	$ 6.350 billion
July–31 Dec. 1976	$ 3.325 billion
Total	$30.212 billion

Allocation of the funds to state and local governments is based on several factors, such as population, relative income per capita, and state and local tax effort. Since these factors can change over time, the allocation of the funds to each unit of government may not be at the same percentage throughout the entire five-year period, although adjustments should be small. Table 1 shows the proposed distribution of the first year's $5.3 billion among the states and their local governments. Approximately one-third is allocated to state governments and two-thirds to local units.

TABLE 1. DISTRIBUTION OF REVENUE-SHARING FUNDS, 1972

State	Total	State Share	Local Share
	In Millions of dollars		
United States, total	5,303.9	1,767.8	3,536.1
Alabama	116.1	38.7	77.4
Alaska	6.3	2.1	4.2
Arizona	50.2	16.7	33.5
Arkansas	55.0	18.3	36.7
California	556.1	185.4	370.7
Colorado	54.6	18.2	36.4
Connecticut	66.2	22.1	44.1
Delaware	15.8	5.3	10.5
District of Columbia	23.6	7.9	15.7
Florida	146.0	48.7	97.3
Georgia	109.9	36.6	73.3
Hawaii	23.8	7.9	15.9
Idaho	19.9	6.7	13.2
Illinois	274.7	91.5	183.2
Indiana	104.3	34.8	69.5
Iowa	77.0	25.6	51.4
Kansas	52.8	17.6	35.2
Kentucky	87.3	29.1	58.2
Louisiana	113.6	37.9	75.7
Maine	31.1	10.3	20.8

State	Total	State Share	Local Share
	In Millions of dollars		
United States, total	5,303.9	1,767.8	3,536.1
Maryland	107.0	35.7	71.3
Massachusetts	163.0	54.3	108.7
Michigan	221.9	74.0	147.9
Minnesota	103.9	34.6	69.3
Mississippi	90.7	30.2	60.5
Missouri	98.8	33.0	65.8
Montana	20.6	6.9	13.7
Nebraska	42.9	14.3	28.6
Nevada	11.1	3.7	7.4
New Hampshire	15.2	5.1	10.1
New Jersey	163.6	54.5	109.1
New Mexico	33.2	11.0	22.2
New York	591.4	197.1	394.3
North Carolina	135.5	45.2	90.3
North Dakota	19.7	6.5	13.2
Ohio	207.0	69.0	138.0
Oklahoma	59.4	19.8	39.6
Oregon	56.2	18.7	37.5
Pennsylvania	274.0	91.3	182.7
Rhode Island	23.6	7.9	15.7
South Carolina	81.5	27.2	54.3
South Dakota	25.1	8.4	16.7
Tennessee	98.4	32.8	65.6
Texas	244.5	81.5	163.0
Utah	31.4	10.5	20.9
Vermont	14.8	4.9	9.9
Virginia	105.2	35.0	70.2
Washington	84.1	28.1	56.0
West Virginia	52.3	17.4	34.9
Wisconsin	133.9	44.6	89.3
Wyoming	9.7	3.2	6.5

Source: Joint Committee on Internal Revenue Taxation

2

The Social and Economic Condition of Rural America

DEMOGRAPHIC TRENDS
OF THE U.S.
RURAL POPULATION

CALVIN BEALE / Economic Development Division, ERS, USDA

> During the last quarter of a century farm machinery, inventive genius, and new discoveries . . . have made it possible for one man to produce four times as much of many farm products as formerly. If a greater percent of the farm boys did not find some other occupation . . . it is evident that there would not be employment for all. . . .
>
> [They see] that three-fourths of the labor formerly required for harvesting . . . crops annually . . . [is] being performed in the cities . . . [by means of] the construction of binders, mowers, harvesting machines, . . . thrashers. . . .
>
> The exodus from the farm was inevitable and justified.[1]

These excerpts sound familiar enough to have been taken from a speech made yesterday by a rural sociologist. Yet, they are from an address by the Director of the Cornell Agricultural Experiment Station in 1896. The migration of people from rural areas has been of concern in the United States for many decades, as this quote indicates. Rural-urban migration first became a prominent issue in the United States with the 1920 census, when it was discovered that the urban population had become larger than the rural population. The present public concern over rural outmigration and urban in-migration is new only in that it pertains to our generation.

Agricultural changes in our nation have caused depopulation

33

in some part of it at practically every stage of our national history, although the total farm population did not reach its peak of 32.53 million persons until 1916. Today, with a total population of over 200,000 million, there are only about 9.5 million people living on farms. The total rural population of about 54 million people represents little more than one-fourth of the total population.

This paper will examine two aspects of the rural population. The first section will be devoted to rural population trends during the 1960–1970 decade. The second section examines some of the causes and effects of rural migration.

POPULATION TRENDS IN THE 1960s

There has been a great deal of internal variation in the population change of the United States in the last several decades. Some of the greatest variations have occurred between the more densely populated urban areas and the relatively sparsely populated rural areas. Two sets of terms are used to describe these areas—urban and rural, and metropolitan and nonmetropolitan. The two sets are not synonymous but are largely overlapping. The rural-urban definition in the census includes all communities of greater than 2,500 population in the urban category, with the population of smaller places and the open country in the rural category. The metropolitan-nonmetropolitan definition, on the other hand, is used to describe the population of entire counties. Metropolitan areas are those counties that contain a city (or twin cities) of 50,000 people or more, plus surrounding counties from which substantial commuting occurs. Similar population trends exist for both definitions, although the metropolitan-nonmetropolitan concept may be more meaningful for program application because of its county basis.

Before examining some of the rural-urban and metropolitan-nonmetropolitan differences in population growth, it is helpful first to note some of the changes in the total population. The population living within the United States, exclusive of armed forces abroad, reached 203 million people in the 1970 census. This represents an increase of 23 million people, or 13.3 percent, over the 1960 population. This is a smaller increase than in the 1950s, when the population grew by 28 million. The lower population increase was brought about from several factors. First, there were about 1.9 million fewer births in the sixties than in the fifties. Concurrently there were 2.6 million more deaths, not because of a deterioration in mortality conditions, but simply because of a larger population at risk, especially larger numbers of older people. Both of these factors worked toward decreasing the rate of the population growth. An offsetting factor was a net increase of 900,000 more civilian immigrants into the United States during the 1960s than during the 1950s.

The total rural population essentially did not change in size. It remained at approximately 54 million. This does not mean that areas that were rural at the beginning of the decade failed to show any growth. Rather, any pronounced amount of growth in a rural area often changed the character of the area to urban, either through annexations by a city or by a town going over the 2,500 mark. The total rural population has in effect remained the same for the last twenty years, although the distribution of people in this category among the different parts of the country has undergone some change.

Turning now to the metropolitan-nonmetropolitan classifications, it can be seen from table 1 that metropolitan counties were gaining in population during the sixties by 16.6 percent, whereas nonmetropolitan counties grew in population by only 6.7 percent. Since the rates of natural increase in these areas are rather similar,

TABLE 1. POPULATION OF THE UNITED STATES BY RESIDENCE, 1950–1970

Year	Population in Thousands	% Change in Previous Decade	Population in Thousands	% Change in Previous Decade	Population in Thousands	% Change in Previous Decade	Population in Thousands	% Change in Previous Decade	Population in Thousands	% Change in Previous Decade
	Total Population		Urban		Total Rural		Rural Farm		Rural Nonfarm	
1950	151,326	14.5	96,847	29.6	54,479	-5.2	23,048	-24.5	31,431	16.8
1960	179,323	18.5	125,269	29.3	54,054	-.8	15,635	-32.2	38,410	22.2
1970	203,166	13.3	149,281	19.2	53,885	-.3	9,712	-37.9	44,173	15.0

Year	Metropolitan		Total Nonmetropolitan		Nonmetropolitan Farm		Nonmetropolitan Nonfarm	
1950	94,711	N.A.	56,615	N.A.	N.A.	N.A.	N.A.	N.A.
1960	119,828	26.5	59,494	5.1	13,029	N.A.	46,465	N.A.
1970	139,707	16.6	63,458	6.7	8,284	-36.4	55,174	18.7

Source: Compiled from reports of the 1950, 1960, and 1970 Censuses of Population, plus estimates of the Economic Research Service.

it is clear that nonmetropolitan areas were unable to retain all of their potential growth and exported a sizeable number of people to the metropolitan areas—a net of about 2.4 million outmigrants. This picture of trends in nonmetropolitan population is only meaningful, however, if it is compared with the previous decade and if it is examined separately for farm and nonfarm people.

In the 1950s, the nonmetropolitan counties grew by just 5.1 percent, while metropolitan areas were increasing by 26.5 percent. Thus during the 1960s, when national and metropolitan population growth slowed considerably, nonmetropolitan growth actually rose somewhat. This rise in nonmetropolitan growth during a period of a falling birth rate reflected a much reduced rate of net outmovement to the metropolitan areas. Although the 2.4 million net loss of people through migration in the 1960s is large in the absolute, it is small in comparison to the 6.0 million net outpouring of nonmetropolitan people into the metropolitan areas during the 1950s. Given the fact that economic factors are the major cause of nonmetropolitan to metropolitan migration, it seems clear that the relative attractiveness of the rural and small-city areas improved during the 1960s.

The improved retention of rural population was not due to any noticeable letup in the migration rate from farms. This rate is estimated to have been about as high in the 1960s (5.0 percent annually) as in the 1950s (5.3 percent). Nonmetropolitan farm population dropped by nearly 5 million people. If the farm population with its pronounced downward trend is subtracted from the total nonmetropolitan population, then one finds that the nonfarm nonmetropolitan population—which includes the great majority of all nonmetropolitan people—rose by 19 percent in the 1960s. This is a rate of growth exceeding not only the national average, but even the metropolitan average.[2] The heavy decline in farm people has masked from public notice the rapid growth of the nonfarm segment of the rural and small-city population.

Because of its long and rapid decline, the farm population now numbers less than 10 million, compared with 30 million thirty years ago. Most of its potential loss has now occurred. It is simply impossible for future outmigration from farms to approach the losses of the recent past. Thus, if nonmetropolitan areas can continue to maintain the conditions that retained and attracted nonfarm people in the 1960s, the overall nonmetropolitan population growth will continue to approach the national average as the influence of farm losses diminishes.

If counties are examined according to their rural-urban composition, it can be seen that their growth rates varied directly in proportion to their urbanization. (See table 2.) Completely rural counties of the United States (without a town greater than 2,500) had almost no aggregate population growth (.1 percent). Population growth increased with urbanization to 15 percent in predominantly urban counties.

TABLE 2. POPULATION CHANGE 1960–1970, AND PRIVATE NON-FARM WAGE AND SALARY EMPLOYMENT CHANGE 1959–1969, BY RURALITY OF COUNTIES IN 1960

Rurality of counties, 1960	Population in Millions 1970	1960	Employment in Millions 1969	1959	Percentage change Population 1960–1970	Jobs 1959–1969
					Pct.	Pct.
U.S. total	203.2	179.3	55.9	41.3	13.3	35.3
Entirely rural	8.2	8.2	1.0	.7	.1	45.5
70–99.9% rural	14.6	13.8	2.4	1.7	6.5	42.2
50–69.9% rural	27.2	24.5	5.6	3.9	10.8	42.3
30–49.9% rural	30.2	26.1	7.2	5.1	15.6	40.7
1–29.9% rural	122.9	106.7	39.7	29.9	15.2	32.8

Counties are grouped according to percentage of population classified as rural in 1960. Percentage of change computed on unrounded data.
Sources: 1970 and 1960 Censuses of Population; 1959 and 1969 County Business Patterns.

Unlikely as it may seem, however, the growth rate of non-agricultural jobs was actually higher in rural counties than in the highly urban group during the 1960s, and highest of all in the completely rural group—a pattern just opposite to that of population growth. Completely rural counties had a growth of 45 percent from 1959 to 1969 in private nonagricultural wage or salary jobs covered by the Social Security system, compared with an average of 33 percent in predominantly urban counties.

This rural job growth failed to bring population growth for three reasons. First, the more rural a county, the smaller the proportion of the labor force working in nonagricultural wage or salary jobs is likely to be. Thus the recent gains in such counties started

37

from a low base and have been readily offset by declines in farm-work. Secondly, many jobs newly taken by rural residents have been going to women, who were previously underrepresented in the rural labor force. These jobs have raised the incomes of many rural households, but jobs for women do not serve to increase the number of families in an area as increased jobs for men do. Finally, much of the increase in nonfarm wages earned by men has gone to former full-time farmers who now must work part-time off the farm to supplement their income. Such part-time work does not contribute to the support of new families, but it may reduce the rate of outmigration.

Regional Population Trends

The trends described thus far are national ones. Emphasis also must be given to the geographic variation in the population growth pattern of rural or nonmetropolitan areas. About 1,350 counties had such heavy outmigration during the 1960s that they declined in population. This, however, is an improvement over the 1950s, when 1,500 counties decreased. For both periods, about five-sixths of the losing counties were rural counties. In the 1960s, more than 1,100 rural counties grew.

Figure 1 shows the counties with population growth and decline during the 1960–1970 decade, while figure 2 illustrates the changes during the 1950s. The declining counties are heavily concentrated in the Great Plains and Corn Belt, the heart of Appalachia, and sections of the Southern Coastal Plain. The great majority of rural counties in the Northeast, the East North Central States and the Far West gained in both the 1950s and 1960s.

Trends in Population Retention

During the 1960s the U.S. experienced a mixture of trends in population retention. Most counties decidedly improved their population retention, but some deteriorated in their ability to hold people, and some continued their previous growth patterns.

The map in figure 3 shows nearly five hundred darkly shaded counties that lost population in the 1950s but experienced enough improvement in population retention during the 1960s to switch from population loss to gain. These turnarounds occurred most often in upland parts of the South. In particular, there has been a remarkable recovery in a large area of northern and western Arkansas and eastern Oklahoma, where outmigration was very severe in the preceding twenty years. Despite a heritage of low average income, low educational attainment, and minimal access to metropolitan-sized centers, this region experienced expansion of industrial, recreational, and retirement enterprises to the point that it ceased to be an area with net outmovement in the 1960s. The lower Tennessee Valley was another area of previously unimpressive socioeconomic status that moved to a position of population growth in the 1960s, based on manufacturing.

The darkly shaded counties in figure 4 lost population in the 1960s after having gained in the 1950s. There were nearly three hundred such counties, most of them located in the Rocky Mountains and the western Great Plains, in the Corn Belt, and along the southern coast.

To sum up the population-change picture for rural or nonmetropolitan areas—it is decidedly mixed. In a way this is regrettable, for hardly anyone likes mixed situations. Certainly not the press, the public, or political leaders. Unrelieved trends are so much easier to comprehend or to take a position on. But the truth of the rural-nonmetropolitan situation is that it is bad in some areas, and not bad in others; worsening in some places but improving in many others. The outmigration from rural and nonmetropolitan areas to the cities is no longer the major source of urban growth, but is still a significant source.

MIGRATION

Some Causes of Rural Outmigration

The causes of migration from rural areas are often complex and dependent on many factors. Three important reasons for the rural-urban migration in this country certainly have been lack of employment opportunities in rural areas, higher standards of living in urban centers, and high rural fertility. The first two causes will be discussed only briefly here, as they are examined in more detail in the next paper on rural problems. The tremendous increase in productivity of farms and the simple fact that a farm operator with modern machinery and capital inputs can now farm much more land than previously have reduced substantially the opportunities for

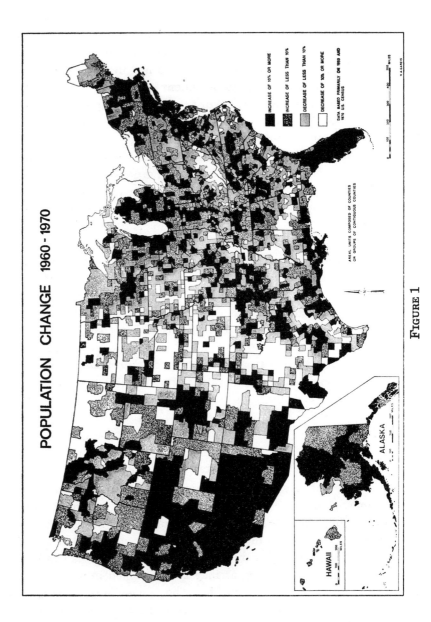

POPULATION CHANGE 1960 - 1970

INCREASE OF 10% OR MORE

INCREASE OF LESS THAN 10%

DECREASE OF LESS THAN 10%

DECREASE OF 10% OR MORE

DATA BASED PRIMARILY ON 1960 AND 1970 U.S. CENSUS

AREAL UNITS COMPOSED OF COUNTIES OR GROUPS OF CONTIGUOUS COUNTIES

ALASKA

HAWAII

FIGURE 1

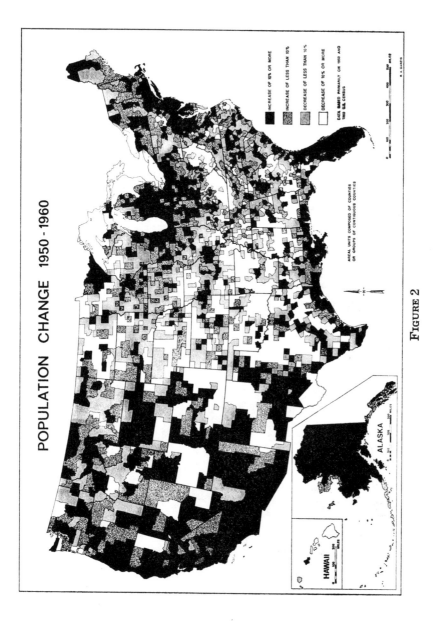

POPULATION CHANGE 1950 - 1960

INCREASE OF 10% OR MORE
INCREASE OF LESS THAN 10%
DECREASE OF LESS THAN 10%
DECREASE OF 10% OR MORE

DATA BASED PRIMARILY ON 1950 AND 1960 U.S. CENSUS

AREAL UNITS COMPOSED OF COUNTIES OR GROUPS OF CONTIGUOUS COUNTIES

ALASKA

HAWAII

FIGURE 2

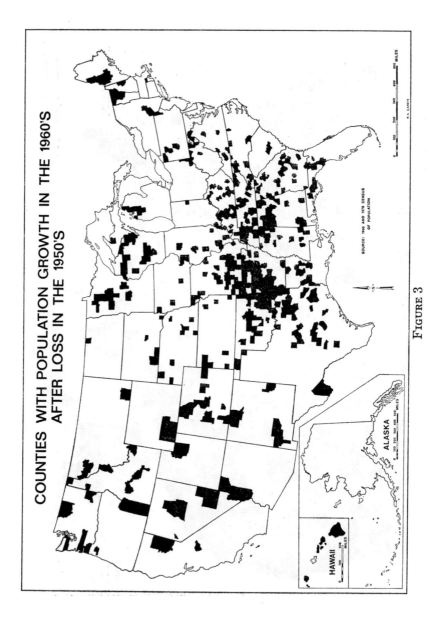

FIGURE 3

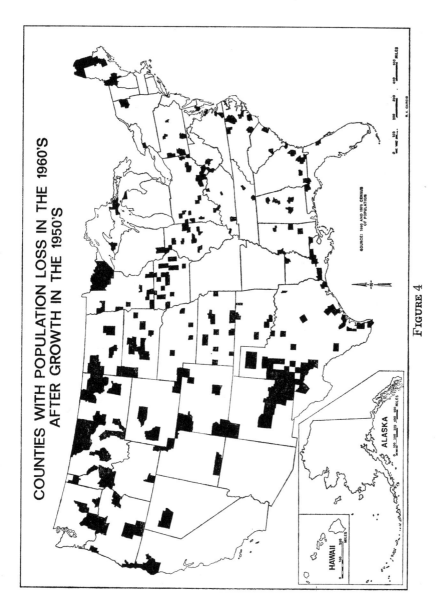

COUNTIES WITH POPULATION LOSS IN THE 1960'S AFTER GROWTH IN THE 1950'S

FIGURE 4

farming. Other factors have been the differences in average income levels available to urban and rural people and the greater variety of job opportunities found in urban areas. Clearly, many young people who have attained a college education must work in urban areas because job opportunities for many types of specialized careers are located only in these areas.

Furthermore, a psychology seems to have developed in rural areas which considers living conditions in urban areas to be superior. Such a psychology tends to equate "urban" with "urbane" and "rural" with "rustic." This attitude is not without some foundation, as many rural communities suffer from shortages of doctors and other professional people, services, retail shopping facilities, adequate housing, and cultural activities.

Rural Fertility

Another cause of rural outmigration, which is perhaps less well understood, is the role of rural fertility. Rural people of the United States have always had larger families on the average than urban people. These large families have created very substantial pressures for outmigration. This outmigration would have been necessary even if the number of farm jobs (or coal-mining jobs in the Appalachians) had not declined. In recent decades, farmers have had enough children to increase their population by about two-thirds in the course of each generation, which is roughly twenty-five to twenty-six years. Many of the groups that have had the heaviest outmigration to the cities, such as the people from the southern Appalachian coal fields, or Negroes from the South, or Mexican-Americans from the Southwest, have had even larger-sized families, enough to double the population of the parent group in each succeeding generation. At this latter rate, it is possible to have a sixteen-fold increase within a hundred years.

In 1960 rural women made up approximately 27 percent of all U.S. women just completing their childbearing (35–44 years old). They had borne, however, about two-thirds of all the children of women in that age group that were contributing to population growth rather than just maintaining the population at a stationary level. To maintain a stable population, about 2,100 children must be born per 1,000 women—1,000 to replace the mothers, 1,000 to replace the fathers, and an extra 100 to account for children who die as infants or before they reach childbearing age. Only the children in excess of these replacement needs serve to increase the population. Each 1,000 rural women have averaged about 950 to 1,000 children above replacement needs in recent years, whereas urban women have averaged only 250 to 300 children above replacement needs per 1,000 women. Consequently, the potential for population increase was at least three times as great per generation among rural women as among urban women. This high growth rate in the rural population has been a major cause of rural-urban migration, particularly when combined with decreasing opportunities for traditional employment in rural areas.

Some Consequences of Rural-Urban Migration

In rural areas, net outmigration is commonly the major component of population change. It is also a principal determinant of age structure. A major consequence of rural outmigration in recent decades has been the high loss of young people from rural areas. From 1950 to 1960 the completely or predominantly rural counties of the United States that had net outmigration lost 40 percent of their youth who reached twenty years of age during that decade. Losses were even higher in some areas—50 percent in the Southern coal-field areas and 60 percent for Negroes in the poorest Southern counties.

There is great variety in the social-economic characteristics of migrants from rural to urban areas. These characteristics are often associated with the migrant's ethno-cultural background and his geographic area of origin. Typically, urban interests welcome white migrants from the Great Plains, the Corn Belt, the Dairy Belt, and even those of the lowland areas of the South, for they are viewed as very desirable workers. Many of these migrants are well educated and come from moderate-income families. The cities, on the other hand, commonly are concerned about the impact of Negroes from the rural South, whites from Southern Appalachian coal fields, Mexican-Americans, and Indians. These groups are viewed as requiring greater social and economic assistance and as being difficult to assimilate. They are characterized by substantial poverty, below-average educational attainment, high social visibility, and relatively large families.

45

Migration, Poverty, and Welfare

Numerous questions have been raised about the relationship between migration, poverty, and welfare. The contention is often made that rural-urban migration is a significant cause of urban poverty. In 1967 a national survey of 30,000 households was undertaken to examine some of the economic and social characteristics of migrants and to compare them with their urban and rural counterparts. This study revealed that approximately 21 percent of the adult urban population, aged seventeen and over, was of rural childhood origin. This group amounted to about 18.5 million people. Interestingly enough, the proportion of the rural population that was of urban origin was nearly the same—23 percent. However, since the rural population is considerably smaller than the urban population, the number of rural residents who were of urban childhood backgrounds amounted to only 8.4 million. Even in nonmetropolitan areas, well beyond the suburbs of large cities, 20 percent of the rural population was of urban origin.

TABLE 3. RURAL AND URBAN CHANGES IN RESIDENCES FROM CHILD-HOOD, FOR PERSONS SEVENTEEN YEARS OLD AND OLDER, 1967

Residents	%	Population Numbers
Urban residents of rural origin	21	18.4 million
Rural residents of urban origin	23	8.4 million

Source: Bowles, Gladys K., "A Profile of the Incidence of Povery among Rural-Urban Migrants and Comparative Populations." Paper presented at the annual meeting of the Rural Sociological Society, August 1970.

Poverty and welfare assistance were also examined in the study to provide comparisons among migrants and urban and rural natives. The measure of poverty used was the federal definition, which varies by size and residence of family. For a nonfarm family of husband, wife, and two children, poverty-level incomes in 1966 were those below approximately $3,400. Table 4 presents the comparisons of poverty and welfare assistance among urban natives and rural-to-urban migrants.

In table 4 it can be seen that there are some differences in poverty and welfare assistance between all urban natives and all rural-to-urban migrants, but these differences are not large. Approximately 9.4 percent of all urban native families were living in

TABLE 4. INCIDENCE OF POVERTY AND WELFARE AMONG URBAN NATIVE AND RURAL-TO-URBAN MIGRANT FAMILIES, BASED ON 1966 INCOME

	Urban Natives	Rural-to-Urban Migrants
	.... % in Poverty	
All Categories	9.4	12.1
Whites	7.4	10.1
Blacks	26.9	26.6
	.... % of Families on Welfare	
All Categories	3.7	5.5
Whites	2.3	4.0
Blacks	15.6	17.3

Source: Bowles, "A Profile of the Incidence of Poverty."

poverty, while 12.1 percent of all rural-to-urban migrants were living in poverty. If these figures are examined by race, it can be seen that the difference was solely in the white population. In the white category, 7.4 percent of the urban natives were in poverty, while 10.1 percent of the rural-to-urban migrants were in poverty. This is a real difference, with statistical reliability, but it is certainly not major in terms of its size.

Within the Negro category, poverty was present among 26.9 percent of the urban native families and 26.6 percent of the rural-to-urban migrants. These two percentages are almost identical. They indicate that blacks have not added to the poverty in cities as rural-to-urban migrants *per se*, but rather as blacks. They have poverty levels that are characteristic of urban blacks, with no indicated additional poverty attributable to their rural background.

Similar relationships exist among urban natives and rural-to-urban migrants for families receiving welfare assistance. Four percent of the rural-urban white migrant families received some welfare income, while only 2 percent of urban native white families received welfare. Of the black families, 17 percent of the rural-urban migrant families were on welfare, while 16 percent of the urban native families were on welfare. It should be noted also that the black families of rural origin had a much lower educational attainment than their urban counterparts. Despite this handicap, the rural-urban migrants achieved incomes that were approximately equal to the urban natives.

These statistics on poverty and welfare are fairly simple, but they should have a substantial effect in reevaluating our notion of what effect rural-urban migration has had on the cities, or what effect cutting back on rural-urban migration might have. Certainly there has been an impact on the cities from the addition of millions of rural people who have migrated to them. This effect, however, does not appear to have been related disproportionately to their rural background, but rather to their race or other characteristics associated with them.

Migration effects on the communities left behind. Most of the attention to the results of rural-to-urban migration has focused on the actual migrants, the migration process, and on the cities to which the migrants have gone. The other side of the picture is the effect on the rural areas that the migrants have left. Unfortunately, these consequences have been greatly neglected in research.

An apparent consequence of rural outmigration, previously mentioned, has been the heavy exodus of youth and the corresponding changes in the age composition of the remaining people. The typical pattern of migration from the Corn Belt or Great Plains has been a very heavy outmigration of young adults at the time they leave high school, with comparatively minor net outmovement of people thereafter. A similar pattern of outmigration has been present among whites in Appalachia, among Southern negroes, and in many parts of Texas, with the difference that the migration has not slacked off among middle-aged or older people as abruptly as elsewhere. Consequently, in these areas the average age is getting somewhat higher, but is not as distorted or as high as in the Great Plains, because more in the older age groups are continuing to migrate. Many counties in Missouri, Kansas, Texas, and portions of Iowa have declined in population in every census of this century, and most of the migrants have been in the younger age brackets.

An example of how the rapid outmigration of young adults from a rural area can effect the age composition is Mills County, Texas. In 1940 the average age in this county was 25. In 1950, when outmigration was getting well under way, the average age reached 35. By 1960 the average age was 45, and it reached 48.7 in 1970, about as high an average as can be found in a county that is not a retirement community.

In many counties of this type, outmigration has distorted the age structure to the extent that more deaths than births are occurring, a phenomenon called natural decrease. From 1960 to 1968 there were some 500 of the nation's roughly 3,000 counties that had experienced more deaths than births in at least one year, simply because there were so few young adults of childbearing age living in them.

Effects of rural outmigration may also be seen in the physical deterioration of many rural communities. One needs only to drive the back roads through the Great Plains or Corn Belt to see the deterioration in small rural towns that has been associated with outmigration. Empty buildings often dot the main street of the towns, which no longer can support the businesses and services of yesterday. In the countryside, numerous abandoned farmsteads attest to the changes in agricultural technology that have caused many people to leave farming. Many larger towns are struggling as the population of their hinterland shrinks and it becomes more difficult to finance services, schools, and other institutions.

There are yet a number of social-economic questions that must be studied and faced as rural outmigration continues. Does rural depopulation, for example, hurt in attracting industry to these communities? What does it do to the local labor force of young workers? How does it effect real estate taxation? To what extent is the population, in which most families have no children in school, willing to support educational facilities? How willing is the government to cope with the needed changes in the community's roads, hospitals, and other public services? Has there also developed a social psychology that is generating continual momentum for outmigration from rural areas? For example, can a young person getting out of high school, who knows that most of his older brothers and sisters and acquaintances have left, retain his own self-respect by staying in the community? Such a psychology may be so deeply developed that it persists even after the circumstances that originally impelled migration no longer exist. Unfortunately, little material is available concerning what socio-economic and psychological effects depopulation has had on these rural communities. Answers to these questions are urgently needed in order to measure the full effects of rural-to-urban migration.

NOTES

1. I. P. Roberts, "The Exodus from the Farm: What are Its Causes and What Can the Colleges of Agriculture Do to Nourish a Hearty Sentiment for Rural Life?" in *Proceedings of the Tenth Annual Convention of the Association of American Agricultural Colleges and Experiment Stations,* Bulletin 41, U.S. Department of Agriculture, Office of Experiment Stations (Washington, D.C., 1897), pp. 80–81.

2. Some of the growth in nonfarm population resulted from reclassification of former farm population due to cessation of farming operations. But this effect is thought to have been a comparatively minor element in nonfarm growth.

SELECTED REFERENCES

Beale, Calvin L. "Rural and Nonmetropolitan Population Trends of Significance to National Population Policy," pp. 665–77 in *Population, Distribution, and Policy,* ed. Sara Mills Mazie, vol. 5 of the research reports of the U.S. Commission on Population Growth and the American Future (October 1973).

———. "Rural-Urban Migration of Blacks: Past and Future," *American Journal of Agricultural Economics,* vol. 53, no. 2 (May 1971).

Bowles, Gladys K. "A Profile of the Incidence of Poverty among Rural-Urban Migrants and Comparative Populations." A paper presented at the annual meeting of the Rural Sociological Society, August 1970. (Available from the Economic Research Service, U.S. Department of Agriculture.)

Fuguitt, Glenn V. "The Places Left Behind: Population Trends and Policy for Rural America," *Rural Sociology,* vol. 36, no. 4 (December 1971).

U.S. Department of Commerce and Department of Agriculture. *Farm Population of the United States: 1971,* Ser. Census-ERS, P-27, no. 43 (May 1972).

U.S. Senate Committee on Government Operations. *The Economic and Social Condition of Rural America in the 1970's.* Committee Print, Ninety-second Congress, 1st sess., May 1971. 141 pp.

THE CONDITION
AND PROBLEMS OF
NONMETROPOLITAN AMERICA

GEORGE BRINKMAN / University of Guelph

During the past century, the United States has been trans-
formed from a predominantly rural to a predominantly urban
society. The cost of that transformation is reflected in the depopulation and the deteriorating community life of many of today's rural
areas and small cities and in our overcrowded, congested large cities.
Though public attention and financial support have been directed
primarily to problems of metropolitan areas, many rural areas and
small cities and towns face more severe problems than do the big
cities. In this paper, we examine causes of deterioration in small
cities and the open country and summarize economic and social conditions to illustrate problems involved in working and living there.

Throughout this paper (as in the preceding paper) "rural"
refers to all open-country areas and cities of less than 2,500 population and "nonmetropolitan" refers to all counties not containing
any city or twin cities of more than 50,000 population. (Likewise,
"urban" and "metropolitan" refer, respectively, to all cities larger
than 2,500 and all counties having a city or twin cities of more than
50,000.) The examining of "nonmetropolitan" areas—which include
both small- to medium-sized cities (2,500–50,000) and "rural" areas
(population under 2,500)—provides a more nearly complete picture
of the plight of small-city residents than could be provided by

examining "rural" areas alone. Although the nonmetropolitan classification is emphasized, the term "rural" and also the phrases "small
cities" or "small cities and rural areas" are used to draw attention to
the small-city and open-country components of nonmetropolitan
counties.

DETERIORATION IN SMALL CITIES AND RURAL AREAS

In the United States the prosperity of rural areas and many
small cities traditionally has depended on a viable agricultural
economy, supported for decades by public policies to improve agricultural production. Agricultural Experiment Stations have developed higher-yielding crop varieties and more efficient farm
machinery. The Extension Service has demonstrated new farming
methods, and land-grant universities have taught technical agriculture to many farmers. Transportation gradually has been improved,
first with railroads and farm-to-market roads, and now with super-
highways. Private companies also have complemented such public
policies by developing new plant and animal varieties, machinery,
and production techniques. All these efforts together have so increased agricultural production that today one farmer feeds an
average of more than forty people, about six times as many as he
fed at the turn of the century.

The dramatic increase in agricultural production and the rapid
technological advances responsible for it, however, have been
primary causes of many problems facing numerous small nonmetropolitan communities. Although it is true that in the early
1970s there have been high food prices and relatively limited supplies of some food commodities; nevertheless, over the past few
decades, agricultural production has generally increased faster than
the demand for food. The relative abundance of farm products has
caused the continual depression of farm prices; and this, in turn,
has pressured many farmers into acquiring more land and adopting
even newer technology in order to maintain their incomes. Many of
the farmers who were slow to adopt new techniques or could not
expand their small farms have gradually been forced out of business, and their land has been acquired by larger farms. As a result,
American farms have become larger in size and fewer in number.
In 1930 there were about 6.3 million farms; by 1960, about 4 million;
and by 1970, only 2.9 million. The total number of large farms,

however, has increased: in 1960 there were 837,000 farms with gross sales of $10,000 or more (representing 21 percent of all farms); by 1970 there were 1,110,000 such farms (or 38 percent of the total number of farms).

With the increase in farm size and the rapid adoption of labor-saving technological improvements, employment opportunities in farming have decreased rapidly. Decreased farm employment, by drastically reducing the economic base of communities, has introduced in many agricultural areas a self-perpetuating spiral of decreasing employment, outmigration, and deteriorating community life. Besides fewer farm workers, there have been fewer opportunities for businesses to provide agricultural services, inputs, machinery, and transportation because of a reduced clientele. Thus, fewer people have been present to support wholesale and retail establishments, professional services, recreational facilities, public institutions, community services, and improvements. Transportation and merchandising developments also have reduced the demand for resources in rural towns, as many rural residents now drive long distances to urban centers to shop and to obtain professional services. The closing down of supporting services and retail businesses in small communities causes further deterioration by making them less attractive places in which to shop and live.

Technological innovations in mineral and logging industries, accompanied by the gradual depletion of natural resources, have created similar problems in cities dependent on the production and processing of coal, oil, lumber, and other raw materials. The depletion of those reserves, along with the time required to replenish timber stands and the increased cost of extracting and processing poorer-quality minerals, has caused the termination of many jobs in mining and lumbering areas. The development of larger, more efficient machines to handle raw materials—such as the gigantic strip-mining shovels with 40-foot-wide scoops—also has reduced employment opportunities in those industries. Such changes, though their overall impact is not so great as those in agriculture, have led to severe deterioration in some cities, adding significantly to the plight of nonmetropolitan areas.

Today many small towns that once flourished as business and trade centers are merely aggregations of low-margin operations—grocery stores, filling stations, taverns, eating places, feed stores, and garages. Vacant store buildings with broken-down fronts line unpaved streets throughout the centers of many such towns. Many residents, including the best-educated people, the best leaders, and especially the youth, are forced to look elsewhere for satisfactory employment and living conditions. With such outmigration, the small cities and rural areas not only lose their leadership, but their institutions also deteriorate (schools, churches, and social, political, and financial organizations), until they are reduced to a size that is too small to operate efficiently. Continued deterioration, accompanied by people moving away, has so shrunk and impoverished many small communities that now they cannot attract doctors, dentists, or lawyers. Many homes have inadequate plumbing, and water and sewer systems often need repair. Yet the deterioration of community buildings and businesses and the outmigration of many residents erode the very tax base that is necessary for public improvements. Without adequate tax revenues for public improvements, the gap in living conditions becomes even wider between residents of metropolitan areas and those of small cities and the open country.

Many residents of small towns have difficulty in finding opportunities to move or cannot move because of their age, their lack of training, or the low salvage value for their life savings, homes, and businesses. Therefore, they often must accept employment in low-paying service operations. Some may be able to commute to urban jobs; but in many sparsely populated areas, major urban centers are so far away that commuting is not practical. Thus, many of those who remain in the small communities are the least successful and least likely to contribute to community development. Poverty is widespread in the small cities and rural areas of America, where half of the nation's poor people live among only 31 percent of the nation's population.

Though nonmetropolitan communities that are considerably isolated from metropolitan areas (especially those quite small) commonly have the greatest community deterioration and most limited opportunities, not all are deteriorating. Some have expanded their economic base from agriculture and have encouraged manufacturing and other primary employment sources. Interested citizens have organized development corporations and community-improvement associations to improve the quality of living and employment opportunities. Such communities, however, are the exception rather than the rule. Today, many small cities and rural areas, particularily those not close to metropolitan areas, are faced with a spiral of declining employment opportunities, outmigration, and deteriorating community facilities.

In the following sections of this paper, I will examine the condition and problems of employment and community facilities in the small cities and rural areas of nonmetropolitan America. (The characteristics of the nonmetropolitan population and problems of outmigration, examined in the preceding paper, will not be analyzed further here.)

NONMETROPOLITAN EMPLOYMENT AND INCOME

For years the rural labor force was considered to be practically the same as "farm workers." Today, however, with the continual decline in agricultural employment over the last few decades, rural areas contain millions of people who have little or no connection with agriculture. Today's nonfarm workers in rural areas and small towns and cities are employed in manufacturing, government, wholesale and retail trade, public and private services, small businesses, and other jobs. Many others are retired, attending school, or in military service. The largest rural occupational group is now the blue-collar segment of the nonfarm work force, which has replaced the traditional groups of farmers and farm laborers.

As shown in table 1, currently the largest source of employment (in terms of earnings) in both metropolitan and nonmetropolitan areas is manufacturing, which accounts for 30.2 percent and 26.8 percent of total earnings, respectively. The second largest source of earnings in metropolitan areas is wholesale and retail trade (17.1 percent), while government is second in nonmetropolitan areas (20.1 percent). Government accounts for 16.0 percent in metropolitan areas; wholesale and retail trade for 14.1 percent in nonmetropolitan areas.

Although farming contributes only a small proportion of total earnings in the U.S., it is still very important in agricultural regions of the United States. Farming contributes about 11 percent of the total earnings in nonmetropolitan areas but only 1 percent in metropolitan areas. It, however, is still the largest nonmetropolitan source of income in the Great Plains (22.6 percent) and is the second largest source of income in nonmetropolitan areas of the Rocky

TABLE 1. EARNINGS BY BROAD INDUSTRIAL SOURCE FOR METROPOLITAN AND NONMETROPOLITAN AREAS, 1969

Broad Industrial Source	Metropolitan		All Regions		Nonmetropolitan % of Earnings within Each Region							
	Millions Dollars	% of Total	Millions Dollars	% of Total	Plains	Rocky Mts.	Southwest	Far West	Southeast	Great Lakes	Mideast	New England
Farming	4,321	.9	15,124	11.0	22.6	16.7	14.5	11.9	9.9	8.3	3.6	3.4
Government	73,627	16.0	27,677	20.1	19.9	21.3	25.3	25.4	19.8	15.8	20.1	21.9
Manufacturing	137,396	29.8	36,871	26.8	14.8	12.0	12.5	18.9	30.3	36.4	33.8	30.9
Wholesale & Retail Trade	78,914	17.1	19,449	14.1	16.1	14.9	13.9	15.2	13.2	14.0	14.1	14.1
Services	72,424	15.7	15,779	11.5	11.3	12.3	11.6	13.3	11.0	10.3	12.5	14.4
Transportation, Communication, & Public Utilities	34,334	7.4	7,291	5.3	5.4	7.1	5.8	5.5	4.7	5.3	5.9	4.6
Contract Construction	29,214	6.3	7,559	5.5	5.4	6.2	5.4	5.4	5.4	5.3	5.7	6.7
Finance, Insurance, & Real Estate	27,580	6.0	3,654	2.7	2.8	2.9	2.8	2.6	2.6	2.5	2.6	3.2
Mining	2,813	.6	3,341	2.4	1.3	6.1	7.6	.8	2.7	1.7	1.2	.2
Total	460,623	99.8	136,745	99.4	99.6	99.5	99.4	99.0	99.6	99.6	99.5	99.4

Source: Survey of Current Business, May 1971, pp. 26–31. States included in Office of Business Economics' regions: *New England*—Maine, New Hampshire, Vermont, Massachusetts, Rhode Island, and Connecticut; *Mideast*—New York, New Jersey, Pennsylvania, Delaware, Maryland, and District of Columbia; *Great Lakes*—Michigan, Ohio, Indiana, Illinois, and Wisconsin; *Plains*—Minnesota, Iowa, Missouri, North Dakota, South Dakota, Nebraska, and Kansas; *Southeast*—Virginia, West Virginia, Kentucky, Tennessee, North Carolina, South Carolina, Georgia, Florida, Alabama, Mississippi, Louisiana, and Arkansas; *Southwest*—Oklahoma, Texas, New Mexico, and Arizona; *Rocky Mountain*—Montana, Idaho, Wyoming, Colorado, and Utah; *Far West*—California, Nevada, Oregon, and Washington.

Mountains (16.7 percent) and the Southwest (14.5 percent). (The states included in these regions are listed at the bottom of table 1.)

Farming is also an important source of income in the Far West, the Southeast, and the Great Lakes region, but its contribution to the total income of the heavily populated areas of the Mideast and the New England states is small. The entire agricultural industry includes much more than just farming, however, and is consequently a more important source of earning than the contributions from farming indicate. In addition to farming, some of the earnings in the categories of government, manufacturing, and wholesale and retail trade can be attributed to agriculture. Local offices of the U.S. Department of Agriculture and the U.S. Extension Service, for example, are sources of government earnings in support of agriculture. The manufacturing of farm machinery and the buying and selling of fertilizers, feeds, and farm products also depend on agriculture for their market or source of supply. In Kansas, for example, 1970 earnings in agribusinesses were nearly three and one-half times as large as those in farming, which was the base for the agribusiness industries. In Kansas, agribusiness and farming together account for about one-third of the total income within the state.

Income in Nonmetropolitan Areas

One indication of the differences in employment and living conditions of metropolitan and nonmetropolitan areas is income earned in each area. Although nonmetropolitan workers now are employed in many of the same kinds of jobs as are metropolitan workers, their income per capita is decidedly lower, as indicated in table 2.

In the various regions, in 1969, nonmetropolitan income per capita ranged from only 67 to 90 percent of the national average and from only 72 to 84 percent of the metropolitan income in the same region (table 2). The nonmetropolitan average income *per capita* for the entire U.S. was only 71 percent of the average metropolitan income, which was a greater difference than found among the individual regions. The apparent inconsistency may be explained by the concentration of nonmetropolitan workers where nonmetropolitan incomes are lowest (in the Southeast) and the concentration of metropolitan workers where metropolitan incomes are highest (in the Mideast, Great Lakes, and Far West). The low-

57

est nonmetropolitan income per capita in all regions, $2,463 in the Southeast, was only 56 percent of the highest regional metropolitan income of $4,374 in the Mideast.

TABLE 2. PERSONAL INCOME PER CAPITA BY METROPOLITAN AND NON-METROPOLITAN AREAS, 1969

Region	Personal Income Per Capita	% of National Average	% that Nonmetropolitan Income is of Metropolitan Income for Each Region
Total U.S.	$3,688	100	
Metropolitan	4,054	110	
Nonmetropolitan	2,871	78	71
Plains			
Metropolitan	3,974	108	
Nonmetropolitan	2,962	80	74
Rocky Mountain			
Metropolitan	3,493	95	
Nonmetropolitan	2,932	80	84
Southwest			
Metropolitan	3,452	94	
Nonmetropolitan	2,753	75	80
Far West			
Metropolitan	4,251	115	
Nonmetropolitan	3,317	90	78
Southeast			
Metropolitan	3,432	93	
Nonmetropolitan	2,463	67	72
Great Lakes			
Metropolitan	4,206	114	
Nonmetropolitan	3,164	86	75
Mideast			
Metropolitan	4,374	119	
Nonmetropolitan	3,325	90	76
New England			
Metropolitan	4,130	112	
Nonmetropolitan	3,211	87	78

Source: Survey of Current Business, May 1971, pp. 20–25.
See table 1 for the list of states included in each region.

Poverty in Nonmetropolitan Areas

Another measure of the economic well-being of nonmetropolitan, compared with metropolitan, areas is the incidence of poverty. Table 3 gives the total number of people in poverty for all of the

TABLE 3. PERSONS BELOW POVERTY LEVEL BY RESIDENCE 1959–1970

Year	All Persons	Metropolitan	Nonmetropolitan
		Persons in Thousands	
1959	39,490	17,337	22,153
1960	39,851	—	—
1961	39,628	—	—
1962	38,625	—	—
1963	36,436	—	—
1964	36,055	—	—
1965	33,185	—	—
1966	28,510	—	—
1967	27,769	—	—
1968	25,389	12,871	12,518
1969	24,280	12,317	11,963
1970	25,520	13,378	12,142
1970	25,520	13,378	12,142
	Percent of Persons in Each Category in Poverty, by Residence		
1959	22.4	15.3	33.2
1960	22.2	—	—
1961	21.9	—	—
1962	21.0	—	—
1963	19.5	—	—
1964	19.0	—	—
1965	17.3	—	—
1966	14.7	—	—
1967	14.2	—	—
1968	12.8	10.0	18.0
1969	12.2	9.5	17.1
1970	12.6	10.2	17.0
	Percent of All Persons in Poverty, by Residence		
1959	100	43.9	56.1
1968	100	50.7	49.3
1969	100	50.7	49.3
1970	100	52.4	47.6

Source: Manpower Report of the President, 19 April 1971; U.S. Bureau of the Census, Current Population Reports, Consumer Income, "Characteristics of the Low-Income Population, 1970," Series P-60, no. 81, November 1971; Special Studies, "Social and Economic Characteristics of the Population in Metropolitan and Nonmetropolitan Areas 1960 and 1970," P-23, no. 37, June 1971; and "Trends in Social and Economic Conditions in Metropolitan and Nonmetropolitan Areas," P-23, no. 33, September 1970.

59

TABLE 4. PERSONS BELOW POVERTY LEVEL IN NONMETROPOLITAN AREAS BY FAMILY STATUS, 1959, 1968-1970

Year	Total Nonmetropolitan Persons in Poverty	Persons in Families						Unrelated Individuals 14 Years of Age and Older
		Total	Heads of Families			Family Members under 18 Years of Age	Other Family Members	
			Total	Nonfarm	Farm			
1959	22,153	19,686	4,718	3,022	1,696	9,293	5,675	2,467
1968	12,518	10,765	2,629	2,135	494	5,257	2,879	1,753
1969	11,963	10,019	2,533	2,105	428	4,789	2,697	1,944
1970	12,142	10,322	2,561	2,125	436	5,080	2,681	1,820

Source: Manpower Report of the President, 19 April 1971; U.S. Bureau of the Census, Current Population Reports, Consumer Income, Series P-60, no. 88, November 1971; Special Studies, "Social and Economic Characteristics of the Population in Metropolitan and Nonmetropolitan Areas 1960 and 1970," P-23, no. 37, June 1971; and "Trends in Social and Economic Conditions in Metropolitan and Nonmetropolitan Areas," P-23, no. 33, September 1970.

TABLE 5. NUMBER OF FARMS AND INCOME BY VALUE OF SALES CLASSES, 1970

Value of Products Sold	Number of Farms	Realized Gross Income Per Farm	Percentage of		Average Net Income			% Off-Farm Income Is of Total Income
			Cash Receipts Received	Government Payments Received	Farm	Off-Farm	Total	
All farms	2,924	$ 19,350	100.0	100.0	$ 5,374	$5,833	$11,207	52
$40,000 and over	223	126,812	52.5	30.4	25,664	5,803	31,467	18
$20,000 to $39,999	374	32,096	21.4	25.5	9,962	3,503	13,465	26
$10,000 to $19,999	513	17,450	15.6	23.7	6,208	3,452	9,660	36
$5,000 to $9,999	370	9,324	5.8	9.1	3,492	4,984	8,476	59
$2,500 to $4,999	260	5,199	2.1	4.1	2,049	5,465	7,514	73
Less than $2,500	1,184	2,148	2.6	7.2	1,059	7,954	9,013	88

Source: Farm Income Situations, FIS 216, Economic Research Service, U.S.D.A., July 1971, tables 1D, 3D-6D, pp. 68, 70-73.

U.S. and their distribution by metropolitan-nonmetropolitan residence for selected years from 1959 to 1970. The poverty definition used here takes into account a range of incomes adjusted by such factors as family size, sex of family head, cost of living, number of children, and farm-nonfarm residence. For example, the 1970 poverty income was $3,968 for a nonfarm family of four and $3,385 for a farm family of four. The lower income range for farm families takes into account the value of home-produced food and provisions.

From table 3 two observations stand out: (1) The number of persons living in poverty has greatly decreased since 1959—by about 14 million persons, or 35 percent; and (2) poverty is more prevalent in nonmetropolitan than in metropolitan areas.

During the 1960–1970 period the total number of people in poverty decreased from 39.9 million to only 25.5 million, an average annual decline of 4.9 percent. For the first time in that period the total number of poor did increase from 1969 to 1970 (by 1.2 million and at a rate of 5.1 percent), but this increase was attributed in part to the slow economy and was expected to be temporary.

The heaviest incidence of poverty is found in nonmetropolitan areas, where nearly half of the nation's poor are found in only about 31 percent of the total population. The majority of the 12.1 million nonmetropolitan persons in poverty in 1970 were white (8.5 million). Of those, about 750,000 to 1 million were of Spanish-speaking origin and often worked as migratory farm laborers in the five Southwestern states of Arizona, California, Colorado, New Mexico, and Texas. The large Anglo white group was concentrated in the Ozarks, Appalchia, and the cutover areas around the Great Lakes. In 1970 about 3.5 million nonmetropolitan Negroes were in poverty, predominantly in the Deep South; the incidence of poverty among nonmetropolitan Negroes was extremely high, 51.6 percent compared with 13.2 for whites. Additionally, those in poverty in 1970 included 158,000 nonmetropolitan persons of other races (predominantly Indians, many on reservations scattered throughout the central and western U.S.). The plight of the Indians, many having very low incomes and poor living conditions, is particularly severe.

Table 4 shows that about 2.5 million nonmetropolitan families were in poverty in 1970. Such families generally are found in small communities, towns, and cities or in the open country rather than

61

on farms; only 16 percent of the nonmetropolitan people in poverty were on farms in 1970.

Agriculture and Community Development

Commercial agricultural policy has been the main form of employment and income assistance to small cities and rural areas for many years. Yet this policy and the network of agencies and programs that support it are insufficient by themselves to promote development in those areas. The major emphasis in commercial agricultural policy has been on commodity programs tied to agricultural production. The benefits of such programs, as well as the benefits from agricultural research and extension, have gone primarily to the large farms. From table 5, which gives the distribution of farms by the value of their sales for 1970, two rather distinct classes of farms emerge: (1) the viable commercial farms with net farm incomes of $10,000 or more and gross sales of $20,000 or more (the farms that have greatly benefited by commercial farm policy); and (2) farms having gross sales under $20,000, down to less than $2,500.

The farms with gross sales exceeding $20,000 account for approximately 75 percent of all cash receipts and 56 percent of government payments received from farming. Yet those farms represent only about 20 percent of the total number of farms. Farms with gross sales less than $20,000 generally produce insufficient income from farm sources to adequately support families at modern living standards. On the average, off-farm income for these farms (some being low-income commercial farms and others part-time, retirement, or abnormal farms) provides the major share of total income, as farm income is significantly low.

The large commercial farms with gross sales of $20,000 or more not only produce significantly more farm income than do smaller farms, but the return per dollar invested in them is generally much higher, as is shown in table 6. Owners of the larger farms (gross sales of $20,000 or more in 1966) had equal or greater returns from their farms per dollar of capital invested and per hour of work by labor than if they had rented out their land and worked elsewhere (landlord standard) or sold their farms, invested the proceeds in common stock, and worked in nonfarm employment (stockholder standard). Operators of smaller farms, however, had significantly lower returns per dollar and per hour of work invested. Farms with $10,000 to $19,999 gross sales yielded returns of 81 to 98 percent of parity under the two standards, while the smallest farms (under $5,000 gross sales) provided returns that were only 31 to 43 percent of parity. Consequently, the small farms not only produced significantly limited farm income, but also used their capital and manpower investments inefficiently. Most small farms simply do not have the quantity or quality of resources to become efficient and to take advantage of current farm programs, which are oriented toward large producers. Many farmers would be much better off out of agriculture, but they have received limited effective help toward making the transition.

The benefits of the production-oriented commodity programs, research, and extension components of our commercial farm policy

TABLE 6. RETURNS FROM FARMING AS PERCENTAGE OF PARITY RETURNS, 1966*

Value-of-Sales Class	Thousands of Farms	Relative Returns under the Landlord Standard**		Relative Returns under the Stockholder Standard**	
		Exclusive of Capital Gain %	Including Capital Gain %	Exclusive of Capital Gain %	Including Capital Gain %
All farms	3,252	81	79	96	82
Farms with sales of					
$20,000 and over	527	129	107	167	112
$10,000 to $19,999	510	85	81	98	84
$5,000 to $9,999	446	62	65	70	67
Under $5,000	1,769	31	43	35	43

* Parity returns measure what the returns to farm labor and capital would have been if they had been used in the nonfarm sector instead of in farming.

** The returns to capital invested in farming under the landlord standard were computed as a percentage of the return that could be realized from renting out the farm (at approximately 6 percent). Under the stockholder standard, the returns to capital were computed as a percentage of the return from investment in common stock. The returns to labor were calculated under both the landlord and stockholder standards as a percentage of the wages that could have been earned in manufacturing, with adjustments for age, education, and sex.

Source: "Parity Returns Position of Farmers," Senate Document No. 44, 90th Congress, 1st sess., August 1967, table 8, p. 22.

also have by-passed the hired farm-work force. In 1970 there were approximately 2.5 million hired farm workers, most of whom were white (78%), male (76%), young (median age 23), nonfarm residents (73%), and nonmigratory (92%).[1] Almost half of the hired farm workers are found in the South (44%), about one-fourth in the North-Central United States, and one-fourth in the West. Table 7, which summarizes the average number of days worked and wages earned by hired farm workers in farm and nonfarm work in 1960 and in the years 1965 to 1970, shows their plight by the low number of days they worked per year and their low daily wage. In 1970 these workers averaged only 80 days of farm work (at an average daily wage of only $11.10) and 46 days of nonfarm work (average daily wage, only $16.35). The average income from all sources for hired farm workers in 1970 amounted to only $1,640, well below the poverty level.

TABLE 7. AVERAGE NUMBER OF DAYS WORKED AND WAGES EARNED PER DAY AT FARM AND NONFARM WAGEWORK, FOR ALL FARM WAGEWORKERS, 1960 AND 1965–1970

	1960	1965	1966	1967	1968	1969	1970
Number of workers (thousands)	3,693	3,128	2,763	3,078	2,919	2,751	2,488
Farm and nonfarm:							
Days worked	122	123	128	121	116	119	127
Wages earned per day (dollars)	6.90	8.55	10.00	10.70	11.60	12.20	12.90
Wages earned per yr. (dollars)	845	1,054	1,279	1,295	1,346	1,453	1,640
Farm:							
Days worked	86	85	85	84	79	78	80
Wages earned per day (dollars)	6.25	7.55	8.55	9.70	10.55	10.75	11.10
Wages earned per yr. (dollars)	537	650	731	817	834	837	887
Nonfarm:							
Days worked	36	38	43	36	36	40	46
Wages earned per day (dollars)	8.50	10.85	12.85	13.25	14.20	15.40	16.35
Wages earned per yr. (dollars)	308	404	548	477	512	616	752

Source: The Hired Farm Working Force, 1960 and 1965–70, Agriculture Information Bulletin 266, 1960; AER nos. 98, 120, 148, 164, 180, and 201, table 7. Economic Research Service, U.S. Department of Agriculture.

Rural and small-city development requires more than just assistance for agriculture, as commercial agricultural policy cannot provide the needed development of human, physical, and capital resources of small communities and small farms. In the past, emphasis has been on agricultural production rather than on human development; therefore, few benefits have gone to farmers on small farms, the hired farm work force, and nonfarm small-city residents. Agriculture, the single largest source of employment in many rural areas, must continue to be supported to keep many small towns viable, but commercial agricultural policy must be complemented with efforts to generate employment for displaced farm workers and nonfarm residents.

We need new policies and programs for small cities and rural areas to develop new nonfarm sources of employment to expand the economic base from commercial agriculture. New sources of nonfarm employment may include industrialization and recreational development and require manpower retraining. The importance of off-farm income in rural areas and small towns is indicated in table 5, which shows that in 1970, 52 percent of all income to farm families came from nonfarm sources. Developing such sources of employment will be even more important in the future, as agriculture's importance continues to shrink.

Successful and Unsuccessful Residents in Nonmetropolitan Areas: A Summary

The residents of nonmetropolitan areas have a great range of incomes and standards of livings. Some of the highest incomes are earned from farming, particularly on large-scale farms having gross sales in excess of $20,000. Other successful farmers include those who, in addition to farming, have substantial nonfarm income. Many nonfarm workers employed in manufacturing, agricultural businesses, and professional services often have good incomes and standards of livings. Numerous people in nonmetropolitan areas, however, have very low incomes and poor living conditions. These include many low-volume farm operators with few agricultural resources and little nonfarm employment. Most hired farm laborers also have substandard incomes, as do many nonagricultural workers who, because of poor training, age, or lack of skills, are unable to obtain satisfactory employment in either farm or nonfarm jobs. The leadership for community development most often will come from the successful group. In their efforts for nonmetropolitan development, they also should consider what assistance and new opportunities they can provide for the group of less successful nonmetropolitan residents.

THE QUALITY OF LIVING IN NONMETROPOLITAN AREAS

An individual's quality of living may be measured by many things: his job, the public and private services he has access to, his cultural activities and living accommodations, the environmental quality, and many other conditions. Although quality of living often is difficult to measure, available evidence readily indicates that nonmetropolitan areas lag considerably behind the metropolitan in many aspects. Major causes of that lag are the relatively sparse population and the low incomes in small cities and rural areas, which commonly make it extremely difficult to support schools and health care and such public services as police and fire protection, water, sewage disposal, and road improvements. The sparsity of population and the low income also affect the quality of private wholesale and retail trade, recreational opportunities, the operation of rural institutions, and a resident's ability to maintain quality housing. Transportation alone contributes heavily to increasing costs, in time and money, for obtaining many amenities in nonmetropolitan areas. Some benefits over metropolitan living may be gained in nonmetropolitan areas from better environmental quality, good friendship, and fewer social pressures. Such benefits, however, often are more than offset by the great cost but poor selection and quality of privately and publicly supplied goods and services. In the next section some differences between metropolitan and nonmetropolitan areas with respect to education, health, and housing are summarized.

Education

Nonmetropolitan residents throughout the United States have shared in the general rise in the educational level in recent years, but they continue to lag behind metropolitan areas in both educational attainment and diversity of educational programs, as shown in table 8. In March 1970 nonmetropolitan areas lagged behind metropolitan areas in educational attainment in all categories of table 8, with the lowest attainment found among farmers and Negroes. In metropolitan areas, 22.1 percent of the white students and 36 percent of the Negro students stopped with eight years of schooling or less, compared to 31.7 and 43.1 percent respectively among nonfarm and farm whites in nonmetropolitan areas, and 59.1 and 74.5 percent respectively among nonfarm and farm Negroes. A comparison of these figures shows that, in nonmetropolitan areas, 43 and 95 percent *more* nonfarm and farm whites (31.7 and 43.1 ÷ 22.1) and 64 and 107 percent *more* nonfarm and farm Negroes respectively (59.1 and 74.5 ÷ 36.0) stopped at the eighth grade than did their metropolitan counterparts. Comparing the percentages of high-school graduates in both areas also shows that only 83 and 68 percent as many non-

TABLE 8. EDUCATIONAL ATTAINMENT OF PERSONS 25 YEARS AND OVER, BY COLOR AND RESIDENCE, 1970*

| | Percent of population with— | | | |
| | 8 years of school or less | | 12 years of school or more | |
Age and residence	White	Negro	White	Negro
Total	26.1	43.0	57.4	33.7
Metropolitan areas	22.1	36.0	61.5	38.8
Nonmetropolitan areas	33.2	60.9	50.0	20.6
Nonfarm	31.7	59.1	51.2	21.6
Farm	43.1	74.5	42.0	11.9
25 to 44 years of age	11.8	22.4	71.6	47.9
Metropolitan areas	9.4	18.0	74.7	52.2
Nonmetropolitan areas	16.5	36.3	65.9	34.2
Nonfarm	15.9	34.3	66.2	35.3
Farm	21.8	54.1	62.3	23.7
45 years of age and over	36.8	63.1	46.6	19.9
Metropolitan areas	32.1	55.7	51.2	24.2
Nonmetropolitan areas	44.9	78.9	38.7	10.5
Nonfarm	43.4	77.9	40.0	11.3
Farm	53.5	86.4	31.9	4.6

* The differences in educational attainment in metropolitan and nonmetropolitan areas reflect the level of attainment by the population currently living in each area rather than the level attained by students in each area. This classification underestimates the level of education taught in nonmetropolitan areas, as many students obtaining high levels of education in nonmetropolitan schools migrate to metropolitan areas and are counted in this category, rather than among the nonmetropolitan category, where they received their education. The data in this table also fail to reflect recent improvements in the educational attainment in nonmetropolitan areas, as only a few of the recent graduates (and almost none of the current students) are over twenty-five years of age and thus are not included in the data.

Source: Manpower Report of the President, April 1971, p. 132.

metropolitan nonfarm and farm whites and only 56 and 31 percent as many nonfarm and farm Negroes graduated from high school. To the extent that higher education contributes to disparities in earning power, nonmetropolitan areas are at a considerable disadvantage. In 1969 the annual-income disparities in nonmetropolitan areas between those people with eight and those with twelve years of education amounted to $1,809; between high school and college graduates, $3,319.[2]

The quality of education in the small cities and rural areas of nonmetropolitan America also is affected by financial support, which is lower than in metropolitan areas. While nonmetropolitan communities have made strong efforts to finance education, their efforts have been limited by their relatively low incomes and by the disproportionately high dependence on property-tax revenue to support schools (which is commonly obtained from a small number of farmers). Transportation also has accounted for a large part of school expenditures, leaving fewer funds for classroom teaching. In 1967–1968 per-pupil teaching expenditures in nonmetropolitan areas (excluding transportation, food service, student activities, and similar costs) were only about three-fourths those of metropolitan areas (roughly $470, compared with $600).[3] Expenditures per teacher have followed a similar pattern. Many small school systems also have less curriculum variety, fewer specialized services, and less laboratory equipment than do the larger school systems of metropolitan areas.

Health

Available data on health services indicate that the more sparsely populated a county is, the more often the residents will have: (1) access to poor-quality health care, (2) a high incidence of serious health problems, and (3) low usage of health-care facilities and services. Those conditions are caused by several factors. Low incomes and sparse populations make it difficult to support the high and rapidly rising costs of modern specialized equipment and highly trained personnel. Low educational levels and great traveling distances also contribute to fewer medical and dental visits and to less use of advice about preventive care, nutrition, periodic checkups, and other measures to reduce illness. Low utilization and low quality of medical services, together with hazardous occupations (particularly mining and farming) and the disproportionate number of elderly persons and children in the rural population, all contribute to a high incidence of serious health problems.

The distribution of hospital facilities and health personnel is given by the degree of urban concentration and rurality of counties in table 9. Generally, rural and nonmetropolitan counties (except in isolated rural areas) have more but smaller hospitals (with nearly the same number of beds per capita) than metropolitan areas have. Unfortunately, many of those hospitals are inadequately staffed, nonaccredited, and lacking in sophisticated equipment and extended-care facilities. The less-populated counties generally have as many general practitioners as do metropolitan counties, but most contain fewer specialists, dentists, and other professionals.

Although the quality of health care in nonmetropolitan areas is relatively low, the need is very great. Table 10 summarizes the incidence of persons with activity-limiting chronic health conditions, such as heart conditions, arthritis, visual impairments, high

TABLE 9. HOSPITAL FACILITIES AND HEALTH PERSONNEL BY COUNTY GROUP, U.S., 1966

	Hospitals	Hospital Beds	Dentists (1964)	GPs		Specialists and Hospital-based Physicians
	Per 100,000 Population					Per 100 Beds
U.S. Average	2.9	381	54	33	92	24.1
Metropolitan						
Greater metropolitan counties (1 million or more inhabitants)	1.8	401	70	34	137	34.2
Lesser metropolitan counties (50,000 to 1 million)	1.9	381	52	28	95	25.0
Nonmetropolitan						
Counties adjacent to metropolitan areas	4.0	323	39	35	38	11.8
Isolated semirural counties (have at least 1 township with 2,500	5.3	412	39	36	46	11.1
Isolated rural counties)	6.3	209	27	33	8	3.8

Source: "Rurality, Poverty and Health," ERS-172, ERS, USDA, February 1970; and "Health Care in Rural America," ERS 451, ERS, USDA, July 1970.

blood pressure, and mental or nervous conditions. Such conditions occur in nonmetropolitan areas about 50 percent more often than in the large metropolitan areas. Infant mortality, another measure of health-care needs, is highest in rural, poverty-stricken counties. From 1961 to 1965, infant mortality in isolated rural areas was 13 percent higher than in metropolitan counties for whites and 30 percent higher for nonwhites.[4] The hazards of farming also contribute

TABLE 10. PERCENTAGE OF PERSONS WITH ACTIVITY-LIMITING CHRONIC HEALTH CONDITIONS, BY PLACE OF RESIDENCE, 1963–1965

Residence	Percent unadjusted for age	Percent adjusted for age*
Large metropolitan areas	9.8	9.8
Other SMSA	11.4	11.9
Outside of SMSA:		
Nonfarm	14.6	14.1
Farm	16.5	15.4

* Adjusted to remove the effects of uneven age distribution among residences.
Source: "Health Characteristics by Geographic Region, Large Metropolitan Areas, and Other Places of Residence," NCHS, Series 10, no. 36, United States, July 1963–June 1965. HEW, Public Health Service, 1967.

significantly to health impairments; farm males lost 18.1 days of work per person per year from all conditions in 1963–1964, compared to 15.3 days for nonfarm-nonmetropolitan males and 13.8 for metropolitan males.[5]

Even though the need for health services is great, nonmetropolitan residents utilize health facilities less than do metropolitan residents. In 1968 nonmetropolitan residents in all age categories had fewer visits to physicians and dentists and lower insurance coverage than did metropolitan residents; farm residents had the lowest number of visits and coverage.[6] Among persons twenty-five years of age and older, for example, metropolitan residents averaged 4.8 physician visits per year, compared to 4.4 visits for nonmetropolitan-nonfarm and 3.9 for farm residents. Farm residents visited dentists only half as often as did metropolitan residents (.7 visits compared with 1.5, with nonmetropolitan-nonfarm residents having .9 visits). More than 86 percent of the metropolitan residents in this age group had hospital-insurance coverage, compared with 81.4 percent for nonmetropolitan-nonfarm and 70.8 percent for farm residents. Many farmers and other rural residents rarely receive sick pay and income-maintenance benefits from their employment, which results in direct income losses whenever they cannot work.

Housing

In 1970 approximately 2.6 million, or 13 percent, of all nonmetropolitan housing units were substandard, compared with 1.8 million substandard units in metropolitan areas.[7] Though these numbers are still substantial, they represent tremendous improvement in housing quality since 1950, when 10.1 million occupied nonmetropolitan units and 5 million metropolitan units were substandard. Incomplete plumbing, one measure of substandard housing, was found in 12 percent of all nonmetropolitan units in 1970, compared with only 3 percent for metropolitan areas. About two-thirds of the nonmetropolitan housing units without complete plumbing were located in the South and one-fifth in the north-central portion of the United States.

Summary of Living and Working Conditions

Nonmetropolitan areas have made substantial improvements in living conditions in recent years, but they still lag considerably behind metropolitan areas. Some of the greatest changes have occurred in life-styles, habits, and attitudes, as mass communications, rural electrification, and faster means of transportation have given nonmetropolitan people easy access to most of the consumer and information sources of metropolitan residents. Today most nonmetropolitan residents have telephones, television sets, electrical appliances, and newspaper service. Good automobiles and improved road networks have also provided them with mobility, so that they can drive to larger cities to obtain services and goods that are unavailable in nonmetropolitan areas. The increased mobility throughout the United States and the widespread use of mass communications have greatly integrated metropolitan and nonmetropolitan areas, bringing the attitudes, consumption patterns, and ways of doing things in the two areas much closer together.

Even though metropolitan and nonmetropolitan life-styles are now quite similar, considerable differences exist between the two areas in income levels and in availability and quality of services and amenities. Employment opportunities in nonmetropolitan areas

71

have greatly diversified from farming to many urban-type jobs, and incomes have shown considerable improvement over earlier years. Nonmetropolitan incomes, however, have remained well below metropolitan incomes. In 1969 the average nonmetropolitan income was only 71% of the average metropolitan income, and the incidence of poverty was almost 70% higher. The lower quality of education, health care, and housing also shows that the standard of living in nonmetropolitan areas is far below the national average. Although there have been improvements in work opportunities and living quality in nonmetropolitan areas in recent years, the development of nonmetropolitan areas has not kept pace with that of metropolitan areas. This lag in development underscores the need for action to correct the imbalance between the nonmetropolitan and metropolitan areas of America.

This paper was written while the author was at Kansas State University. It is Contribution No. 488 of the Department of Agricultural Economics, Kansas Agricultural Experiment Station.

NOTES

1. Robert C. McElroy, *The Hired Farm Working Force of 1970*, AER no. 201, Economic Research Service, U.S. Department of Agriculture (March 1971), table 4, pp. 10–12.
2. U.S. Bureau of the Census, "Social and Economic Characteristics of the Population in Metropolitan and Nonmetropolitan Areas: 1970 and 1960," *Current Population Reports*, ser. P-23, no. 37 (Washington, D.C.: U.S. Government Printing Office), table 12, p. 54.
3. Economic Development Division, Economic Research Service, U.S.

Department of Agriculture, *The Economic and Social Condition of Rural America in the 1970s* Washington, D.C.: U.S. Government Printing Office, May 1971), p. 105.
4. Ibid., p. 85.
5. Economic Research Service, U.S. Department of Agriculture, *Health Care in Rural America*, ERS 451 (July 1970), p. 3.
6. Economic Development Division, *The Economic and Social Condition*, pp. 86–91.
7. Ibid., pp. 107–11.

BIBLIOGRAPHY

Hanson, Niles. *Rural Poverty and the Urban Crisis*. Bloomington, Ind.: Indiana University Press, 1970.

Hathaway, Dale E. *Government and Agriculture*. New York: The Macmillan Co., 1963.

Nixon, Richard. "Reorganization of the Federal Government." Message from the President of the United States to the House of Representatives. *Congressional Record,* House, H2022, 25 March 1971.

"Personal Income in Metropolitan and Nonmetropolitan Areas," *Survey of Current Business,* vol. 51, no. 5 (May 1971).

President's Task Force on Rural Development. *A New Life for the Country.* Washington, D.C.: U.S. Government Printing Office, March 1970.

Tweeten, Luther. *Foundations of Farm Policy.* Lincoln, Nebr.: University of Nebraska Press, 1970.

U.S. Advisory Commission on Intergovernmental Relations. *Urban and Rural America: Policies for Future Growth.* Report A-32. Washington, D.C.: U.S. Government Printing Office, April 1968.

U.S. Bureau of the Census. *Current Population Reports.* Ser. P-60, no. 81. "Characteristics of the Low-income Population, 1970." Washington, D.C.: U.S. Government Printing Office, 1971.

———. *Current Population Reports.* Ser. P-60, no. 77. "Poverty Increases by 1.2 Million in 1970." Washington, D.C.: Government Printing Office, 7 May 1971.

———. *Current Population Reports.* Ser. P-23, no. 37. "Social and Economic Characteristics of the Population in Metropolitan and Nonmetropolitan Areas: 1970 and 1960." Washington, D.C.: U.S. Government Printing Office, 1971. Table 12, p. 54.

———. *Current Population Reports.* Ser. P-23, no. 33. "Trends in Social and Economic Conditions in Metropolitan and Nonmetropolitan Areas." Washington, D.C.: U.S. Government Printing Office, 1970.

U.S. Department of Agriculture, Economic Development Division, Economic Research Service. *The Economic and Social Condition of Rural America in the 1970s.* Washington, D.C.: U.S. Government Printing Office, May 1971.

———. *The Hired Farm Working Force of 1970.* AER 201, by Robert C. McElroy. Washington, D.C.: U.S. Government Printing Office, March 1971.

———. *Rurality, Poverty and Health.* AER 172, by Neville Doherty. Washington, D.C.: U.S. Government Printing Office, February 1970.

———. *Rural People in the American Economy.* AER 101. Washington, D.C.: U.S. Government Printing Office, October 1966.

U.S. Department of Agriculture, Economic Research Service. *Farm Income Situation.* FIS 218. Washington, D.C.: U.S. Government Printing Office, July 1971.

———. *Health Care in Rural America.* ERS 451. Washington, D.C.: U.S. Government Printing Office, July 1970.

U.S. Department of Health, Education, and Welfare, National Center for Health Statistics, Division of Health Interview Statistics, Public Health Service. *Health Characteristics by Geographic Region, Large Metropolitan Areas, and Other Places of Residence, United States, July 1963–June 1965.* Ser. 10, no. 36. Washington, D.C.: U.S. Government Printing Office, 1967.

U.S. Department of Labor. *Manpower Report of the President.* Washington, D.C.: U.S. Government Printing Office, April 1971.

U.S. Senate, 90th Congress, 1st sess. *Parity Returns Position of Farmers.* Document 44. Washington, D.C.: U.S. Government Printing Office, August 1967.

3

Rural
Development
Alternatives

SYSTEMS PLANNING FOR RURAL DEVELOPMENT

LUTHER TWEETEN / Oklahoma State University

INTRODUCTION

Planning for rural development entails *strategy* and *tactics*. The strategy encompasses development planning and appropriate public policy. The tactics deal mainly with implementation of strategy and are oriented frequently toward issues of community power structures, leadership, and organization. Both strategy and tactics are essential for development, and the systems approach can be used in either, although this paper deals only with development strategy.

I describe the systems approach to planning, then outline a linear programming model that can be used as one tool for comprehensive policy planning in the systems framework. Much of this paper deals with data available from past studies on the cost effectiveness of individual programs which can form the foundation for systems planning. The data are not yet adequate for comprehensive systems planning but are of interest in themselves—they provide initial guidelines for setting program priorities to reach development targets efficiently. The analysis should interest national policy planners. Where an adequate set of programs is available, it can also help community leaders and development practitioners choose which ones to stress at the local level; and where an adequate set of programs is not available, what programs to "lobby" for in new public policies and legislation.

Regional development programs (including related public-assistance and manpower programs) have expanded markedly in recent years. Federal funds for community and regional development tripled between 1960 and 1968, when they totaled $36.6 billion.[1] The number of first-time enrollees in federally assisted work and training programs was nominal in 1960, .3 million in 1964 and 1.5 million in 1968. Enrollment in largely state-operated but federally aided programs of vocational-technical education totaled 3.8 million in 1960 and 7.5 million in 1968. Public-assistance payments from all sources totaled $3.8 billion in 1960 and $9.8 billion in 1968 (U.S. Department of Commerce, 1970, p. 297). This report will be documented by a number of studies that analyze the economic payoff from these and related programs.

Many of the national programs of community and regional development apply simultaneously to rural and urban areas. In some programs, rural people receive a disproportionate share of the benefits; in others, urban people receive a disproportionate share (Coffey, 1971). To reach development targets, rural areas may wish to press for a redistribution of funds among programs or for more funds in total. Economic evaluation of the efficiency of the various programs, viewed in the context of systems planning, can help rural people decide which programs to expand and which to contract and what total level of funds is required to reach development targets. Previous studies have not considered the many possible programs for economic development as part of a comprehensive system with interactions and linkages. The shortcomings of legislation and inadequate planning have resulted in many fragmented, inefficient, and overlapping programs. This paper shows how systems planning can be used to devise an efficient rural-development strategy.

SYSTEMS PLANNING

The term "general systems theory" (von Bertalanffy, 1951) has been in the literature for some time. Systems planning is not new, but placing a man on the moon has dramatized its effectiveness in solving problems and reaching an objective. Systems planning is not a technique; it is a systematic way of solving problems. To the extent that it represents the common sense that any good researcher uses in solving problems, systems planning is as old as problem-solving itself.

Defining the Systems Approach

No single, concise definition describes the systems approach, but the method of solving problems does have certain more or less accepted characteristics:

1. Recognition of the total problem: all parts of the phenomenon in question that bear significantly on the solution must be accounted for within the system.

2. Each component or subsystem must be understood in its relationship to other subsystems and the total system. The problem solution must recognize time sequences and must mesh the components properly in reaching the chosen target(s).

3. The system must be tied together by communication networks and other linkages.

4. The process must be monitored for efficiency. Cost-effectiveness, benefit-cost analysis, program planning and budgeting, and other terms describe the evaluation techniques.

5. The performance of the system must be evaluated in relation to the targets or objectives, with feedback to adjust the process in accordance with information gained from experience. Quantitative approaches such as simulation and programming are often used to gain "experience" through small-scale operation of the system. The study of the control mechanism for the system is sometimes called *cybernetics*.

Each of the first four elements in systems planning is discussed in sequence below, following a brief examination of objectives and targets.

Objectives and Targets

One reason for the success of the moon program was that it had a well-defined objective—a man on the moon by 1970. Rural development has not had such a well-defined goal. Because public funds to promote rural development are limited, it is important that they be used efficiently. The objective of rural development could be conceptualized as maximizing net income of a population or region that has limited public funds available for programs to promote development. Or the objective might be to minimize the public cost of reaching certain development targets. These development targets might be desired levels of employment, income, and stability. A goal in the systems approach might be to reach targets by a designated year at the lowest public expense while maintaining at least a poverty-threshold income for the poor. The focus is on efficient use of public funds, but private investment is frequently complementary. In fact, public funds are likely to be most effective in raising incomes where they induce considerable private investment.

Recognizing the Total Problem: A Programming Model

One of the several possible models for devising a development strategy in the systems context is linear programming. The objective function (1) expresses the total public cost, Z, as a function of the specific program level, x_j, times the public cost per unit of that program, c_j. In matrix notation:

(1) Min $Z = C X'$

where C and X are row vectors of c_j and x_j respectively. Constraints in the system are designated by a column vector, B. The row constraints, b_i, include the number of the population in various demographic and work-eligibility categories and the income and other targets for a specific category. The "technical" coefficients, a_{ij}, indicate the impact of public policy, j, on the subsystem population in row i. The public cost, Z, is minimized subject to constraints that income and other targets be equal to or greater than prescribed levels as in (2),

(2) $AX' \geqq B$

where A is the matrix of technical coefficients. The final constraint is that the public-policy activities be at non-negative levels:

(3) $x_j \geqq 0$.

Linear programming is one possible formulation: Dynamic, poly-period, or nonlinear programming might improve the model. Simulation techniques could provide even more flexibility and allow analysis of the system over an extended period of time. Simulation with population cohorts could reflect the impact in subsequent generations of, for example, family-planning policies in the current generation. Experimentation with various models could reveal

80

which formulation is best suited to devise a rural-development strategy.

A comprehensive system comprising all population subgroups in the U.S. (or the world!) would be conceptually ideal, but opererationally unmanageable. A smaller system is essential, and there are no objective guidelines for optimal size. One delineation is to include within the system all in this nation who are in poverty (and near poverty), recognizing that errors will arise because poverty programs influence persons outside this system. Another approach is to include the entire population within a region, recognizing that errors will arise because programs for a region will influence persons in other regions. The geographic unit chosen for economic-development planning ordinarily will encompass at least a multicounty economic-development district or a multidistrict region, such as the Ozarks. The county, township, or town unit is too small for devising a development strategy if changes in national public policy are an issue.

Recognizing Subsystems, Timing, and Interactions

As stated earlier, an advantage of the systems approach is that it can find the optimal combination of programs that will use limited public funds efficiently while meeting targets geared to unique characteristics of a heterogenous population. To see the importance of recognizing subsystem diversity, it is only necessary to review characteristics of the poor. Of the 11 million households in poverty in 1966, (a) 39 percent were characterized by an aged head (65 years and over), (b) 27 percent by a female head under 65 years of age (over 80 percent included at least one child under 18, and over half included at least one child under 6 years of age), (c) 4 percent by a head that was ill or disabled, (d) 22 percent by a male head employed full-time, and (e) only 8 percent by an able-bodied male head employed sporadically or not at all. Welfare programs with built-in work incentives apply particularly to group (e). Income of aged and disabled groups (b) and (c) may be raised most efficiently by transfer payments, while training programs to upgrade skills may be the most efficient use of public funds to lift incomes of those poor (d) who are fully employed. Emphasis in early years might be on programs of the public-assistance type until programs that rank higher in long-term cost-effectiveness, such as family

81

planning, induced migration, and education, have had time to realize their impact.

Industrial-location incentives, long-term land retirement, and general education may efficiently raise regional income, but they are frequently regressive in character—that is, they disproportionately concentrate benefits on those who least need special public help. There is a fundamental conflict in programs between equity (favorable distributional effects) and efficiency. With few exceptions, programs that make limited public funds go farthest to raise incomes go to individuals who would have succeeded (because of above-average drive and ability) in the absence of such programs.[2] The disadvantaged are left out of programs if efficiency is pursued without regard to equity. This problem can be handled in the design of a programming model having an objective function that maximizes income of a region. The population is merely divided into various categories and the stipulation made that income attain at least some minimum level for the most disadvantaged. The shadow prices indicate the loss in aggregate income in the entire system stemming from such a stipulation. The results thus can quantitatively illustrate the trade-off between efficiency (maximum aggregate income from program budget) and equity (favorable distribution of income).

Communication Networks and Linkages

The complexity and diversity of public programs to promote regional economic development heightens the need for communication and linkages among programs. A program of the family-assistance type would call for even stronger linkages. The federal-state employment service, vocational-technical training programs, and organizations administering welfare programs are key elements. The employment service has been increasingly active in referring the hard-to-employ to manpower training programs. And welfare agencies are increasingly active in referring persons to rehabilitation programs. Some types of linkages between employment, training, and welfare programs can be handled by appropriate specification of a quantitative systems model.

Data from the Work Incentive Program (WIN) at once illustrate the importance of communication and linkages among programs and the difficulty in quantification. WIN, established by the

1967 amendments to the Social Security Act, has the goal of economic independence for all employable persons age sixteen or over in families now receiving Aid to Families with Dependent Children. Enrollments were expected to reach 150,000 by the end of fiscal 1971, making WIN one of the largest manpower programs. Nevertheless, it will be several years before WIN, or any other successor program, can enroll the entire target population—the estimated 1.1 million adults on welfare rolls for whom jobs and job training are possible avenues to self-sufficiency. The WIN program, though extensive, has almost totally eluded rural areas (Coffey, 1971, p. 12).

The WIN Program is administered by the Department of Labor through state employment agencies. Local welfare agencies refer clients to employment-service offices for interviewing, testing, counseling, and placement in jobs, job training, or special work experience, depending on the degree of job readiness. Stress is on helping clients to obtain meaningful jobs as rapidly as possible—at not less than the minimum wage or the prevailing wage, whichever is higher. All WIN enrollees receive their welfare bentfits plus some training incentive payments. Welfare agencies continue to supply supportive medical and social services, including day-care centers for children.

In its early phase, the WIN Program has encountered a number of problems. In particular, there is a shortage of day-care arrangements for children in most areas where the program is operating. Quality day care is scarce and expensive. The Department of Health, Education, and Welfare estimates the cost of after-school and summer care for school-age children at $400 per child per year, and for full-day care for preschoolers at $1,600. These data suggest that the cost of day care severely reduces the cost-effectiveness of work-training programs for welfare mothers with preschool children, and could eliminate the program for such mothers from a cost-effective rural-development strategy.

Monitoring Efficiency in a System

Cost-effectiveness refers to efficient use of available means to reach a given objective. It can be expressed in several ways. Nearly all expressions recognize that public funds to promote regional development are severely limited. One of the simplest concepts is the amount of public funds required to create a permanent new job. Another concept is the income generated in a region per dollar of public funds spent to promote economic progress. A broader concept is the net income generated in the nation per dollar of public and induced private expenditures in a given region. Benefits in the form of income generated in the region ideally should be adjusted for income changes in other regions. Income generated by publicly induced industrialization of a depressed area may mean loss of jobs to communities where some industry would otherwise have located. And programs to enhance mobility in a region may generate income in other regions by outmigrants. Another cost-effectiveness concept is the reduction in the incidence of poverty per dollar spent on a program. A criterion suggested earlier for linear programming was to maximize income per public dollar spent in a region, subject to the stipulation that the income of each subgroup must attain at least the poverty threshold.

Regional-development programs, like fertilizer application, cannot elude the law of diminishing returns. Injection of public funds into a program that has high cost-effectiveness will eventually drive efficiency down to a point where other programs will better utilize incremental public outlays. This principle, coupled with uncertainty and the need to reach special groups, leads to diversification of funds among programs.

The principle of diminishing returns is illustrated by data for 1959 from Hines and Tweeten (1972, table 1), which indicate that a $100 increase in direct schooling outlays per student reduces the marginal rate of return on schooling by 1.19 percentage points.

Diminishing returns influence supply; other factors influence demand. If the program is large enough to have a perceptible macro effect, the declining demand curve must be considered. Plans for a small development district may require few adjustments for declining prices as output is expanded through development programs. Plans for a large region that accounts for a major portion of the output of an industry would require more adjustments for declining prices.

Essentially, the systems approach is to first introduce the program that will contribute most to income per public dollar spent. If this program encounters diminishing returns or declining prices or does not reach specific groups such as the poor, then a new program is introduced to supplement or replace the first program. This process is repeated until the objective function is optimized, subject to constraints that must be met. The process cannot easily be performed by trial-and-error budgeting. The interactions, programs, and subsystems are too numerous and complicated. But the simple cost-effectiveness estimates that will be presented later do give some first approximations, which can help set program priorities until more refined estimates are available.

The a_{ij}'s ("technical" coefficients) should reflect efficient use of a given program. In general, a program such as industry-location incentives will be most efficient if directed toward city units of efficient size. This topic—the efficient size of units on which to focus development programs—is sufficiently important to warrant attention in the following section.

WHERE TO FOCUS DEVELOPMENT PROGRAMS

Current policies are not adequate to bring satisfactory levels of living to rural areas. The necessary transformation requires new policies and new planning as well as local leadership. Before embarking on bold new policies, it is essential to confront the issue of where economic and population growth should occur in the system.

To avoid wasting the energies of those working to achieve rural development, there are certain realities that must be faced. One is that the exodus from the farm will continue, although the absolute number of farm-urban migrants will drop substantially. In the 1970s, only one in four Oklahoma farm boys reaching the age of employment can find an adequate farming opportunity (Lu et al., 1970). It is estimated that no more than one in five farm boys in the U.S. can find an adequate farming opportunity in the same period.

Not every rural town can grow. Most small towns will be unable to retain the majority of their young people seeking jobs, and many will decline in population. Comparatively few small towns can attract industry—there simply are not enough industrial plants or other job-creating opportunities to go around.

To understand why every town cannot attract an industrial plant, it is well to review briefly what industry seeks in a location. One factor is the availability of adequate transportation facilities: interstate highways, rail transportation, and a major airport. Another factor is nearness to markets: most industries directly or indirectly produce for consumers, and this means they want to be near large numbers of people. A third factor is adequate inputs,

85

including raw materials and labor supply, both in the number and quality of workers. This frequently requires locating near like industries in order to purchase inputs from common suppliers and to be aware of changes in industry styles and technologies. Specialized labor skills are required in progressive industries. Many of the best-paying firms, to achieve economies of size, must employ large numbers of people in a single plant. Finally, firms look for adequate community services, including schools, utilities, financial institutions, health services, and churches; many rural communities cannot supply these along with progressive community attitudes toward change.

Many small communities faced with a shortage of these attributes must compensate a locating industry with subsidies in the form of low-interest loans, property-tax exemptions, free or low-cost land and buildings, and low-wage labor. These compensations can severely burden the community. Industrialization does not bring unmitigated benefits to a rural community. It may increase social problems and taxes (even for residents who do not benefit), overburden services, cause pollution, and even turn the community's power structure over to "outsiders." The benefits to local workers from a new plant are reduced by bringing in skilled workers from outside and by the one-shot employment effect. That is, without a series of new plants and sustained employment growth, the community continues to lose its young people after the initial employment requirements of the new plant have been met.

Metropolitan America will contain an increasing proportion of the nation's population in the 1970s. Currently, 70 percent of the nation's population resides in metropolitan communities. These communities, defined as cities of 50,000 or more and their surrounding towns, accounted for three-fourths of the nation's growth in the 1960s. Urbanization inexorably attends economic growth. But there is considerable evidence that it can go too far. Our large metropolitan areas are plagued by serious problems of air pollution, congestion, crime, and violence. Many of the costs associated with these problems do not enter the private accounts of firms asking location decisions; hence firms find the metropolis profitable, and jobs and people continue to flow in.

Others must pay the cost, including rural residents. Antipollution and other programs are attempting to make the metropolis more livable. Policies that require the use of nonlead gasolines and of devices for controlling exhaust emission presumably will apply to all residents, although air pollution by motor vehicles is not a problem in rural America. Calculations suggest that despite few benefits to them, the cost of such policies to rural residents is not small. The added cost of the control package—higher gasoline prices, loss of power, and engine modifications—amounts to $680 per car on a ten-year basis. If the annual cost of $68 is multiplied by 20 million cars owned by rural residents, the annual cost to rural residents of helping to control metropolitan smog is over $1 billion.

The problems cited above of the large metropolis suggest that it is not a logical place to promote the location of new jobs and more people. The declining number of jobs in agriculture and mining coupled with the disadvantages cited earlier of small towns in attracting new jobs suggest that efficient efforts to promote development would not concentrate on the small town. It appears that programs for using limited resources to promote a more nearly optimum distribution of jobs and people, consistent with economic and social efficiency, should focus on cities between these extremes in size.

After adjusting cities of all sizes to comparable characteristics and varying only city size, one study (Morris and Tweeten, 1971) estimated that the cost per capita of controlling crime in cities with over one million inhabitants is approximately twice the cost of controlling crime in smaller cities. Research on economies of city size, which is being done by people at Oklahoma State University as well as by others, indicates that the cost per capita of providing adequate public services tends to be lowest in cities ranging from roughly 20,000 to 1 million in population. On the other hand, economic vitality, as measured by a dynamic and growing job market, tends to be highest in cities of 200,000 or more residents. So growth centers may be as small as 20,000 if no other centers are within commuting distance, but ideally should be larger—though not over 1 million population. The coefficients for the systems model described earlier should reflect growth strategies focused on cities of optimal size.

The concept of having an adequate growth node or center was embodied in the Public Works and Economic Development Act of 1965, which provided for economic-development districts. These districts tend to contain at least one city of 20,000 or more population, which serves as a growth node. These cities, generally within commuting distance of rural residents, should be sufficiently viable and should have proper policies in order to provide new jobs to compensate for declining job opportunities in other parts of the district. There are advantages also in planning for medical and health facilities, vocational schools, and other public services in regions of this size. Although the county often is not an adequate-sized unit for planning and provision of services, this does not necessarily call for consolidation of rural counties. There appear to be few net economies in government due to size for counties with a population of over 10,000. Savings from consolidation of county functions are offset by higher transportation costs for people who drive to the county seat and for county officials who drive to the people (Klindt and Braschler, 1969).

THE DATA

Shortcomings of data currently preclude realistic empirical applications of the "sophisticated" systems planning described earlier, which simultaneously recognizes diminishing returns, interactions, time lags, subsystems, and efficiency. However, the conceptual framework outlined gives direction to future planning, and it highlights data gaps. These gaps are slowly being filled in as the result of emphasis on individual program planning and evaluation in recent years. Considerable benchmark data are available on several programs; these can provide initial estimates of the a_{ij}'s, b_i's and c_j's.[3]

Much of the remainder of this paper enumerates results of past studies of actual or potential public policies to promote development. The results, while providing some coefficients for the models described earlier, are also of interest in themselves by suggesting priorities for programs that make public funds go far in raising income and levels of living. Viewed as separate and distinct entities, the studies fail to tell what combination of programs will reach specific policy targets at minimum public expense and what time interval and public expense are needed to reach the targets. Cost-effectiveness measures do not show optimal output, that is, how far to pursue a given objective.

Since major public concern is focused on the economic position of persons in the lower income brackets, much of the following discussion of programs is oriented to this group. The available studies that provide cost-effectiveness measures are not oriented to a single criterion of efficiency. For the first two programs—family planning and national full employment—reduction in the incidence of poverty is the criterion. For the subsidized migration, education, and training programs, the social rate of return on investment is the criterion. For subsidized private and public employment and for industry-location incentives, the public cost per job created is the criterion. Finally, for public-assistance and farmland-retirement programs, the increment in income per public dollar spent is the criterion. Each of these programs is discussed below.

Family Planning

Surveys indicate that "poor women want no more children than nonpoor women have, and perhaps fewer," according to Kershaw and Courant (1970, p. 60). They estimate that if poor families had the number of children they wanted, there would be 450,000 fewer poor children born each year, and many families would move above the poverty line because of being smaller. They estimated that it would cost $20 per woman per year to supply family-planning devices and advice. With approximately 5 million poor women of childbearing age, the cost would be $100 million if they all took advantage of family-planning help, though of course not all would. These estimates by Kershaw and Courant (1970, pp. 60–61) imply that the cost-effectiveness of family planning is very high, not much over $200 to reduce the number of persons in poverty by one. Though this figure is undoubtedly on the optimistic side, even a substantial allowance for error leaves this program at or near the top of the cost-effectiveness category in meeting one development target—reduction of the number of persons in poverty. Other studies by family-planning organizations (cf. Jaffe, 1968, chap. 21) and by Bogue (1968, chap. 22) provide additional data.

Full Employment

Public monies, in conjunction with induced private investment, go far to raise the income and well-being of rural people when spent on monetary and fiscal policies for full employment. Monetary policies for full employment entail comparatively little opportunity cost and hence have a high social benefit-cost ratio. The issue remains:

Do such policies really help the poor, that is, is the distribution of benefits from such policies progressive or regressive?

One study used the "trickling down" hypothesis to analyze the change in the incidence of poverty among farm families under various assumptions of national unemployment (Madden, 1968). Assuming a 4 percent national unemployment from 1966 to 1975, the incidence of poverty among white farm families was projected to fall from 28 percent in 1966 to 20 percent in 1975. The incidence of poverty among nonwhite farm families was projected to fall from 75 percent in 1966 to 67 percent in 1975 under the same national unemployment percentage. The incidence of poverty by 1975 was nearly the same when a 6 percent national unemployment rate was assumed. In 1966 nonwhite farm families were so far below the poverty threshold that it would have taken considerable economic progress to have moved even a very few above the $3,000 threshold used by Madden. Thus full-employment policies would not be as effective as one might expect in reducing the incidence of poverty.

But the poor who are "last hired and first fired" are sensitive to changes in national employment. Furthermore, the success of nearly all positive policies directly focused on the rural poor depends on the availability of jobs. It does little good to provide job counselors, employment bureaus, and training centers if jobs do not exist.

National monetary policies for establishing full employment are not by themselves sufficient to eliminate rural-urban income differences and poverty in a reasonable period. Once national unemployment is down to about 4 per cent of the labor force, other programs become more efficient means of improving the economic position of rural people.

Fiscal policies for full employment can have widely different effects, depending on where public funds and programs to stimulate employment and incomes are focused. The remainder of this chapter examines a number of fiscal policies.

Improving Labor Markets: Bringing People to Jobs

Much research has described the mobility of rural people, particularly farm workers (cf. Hathaway and Perkins, 1968). In contrast, very little research has focused on improving the mobility of labor, though lack of such mobility is considered one of the key elements explaining chronic low returns on labor resources in rural areas. Migrants rely primarily on information from friends and relatives to learn about availability of jobs. We know very little about the delivery of job information to rural people by the Federal-State Employment Service.

The employment service potentially could provide various degrees of assistance to potential job-seekers, including: (1) a continuation of present practices, (2) additional job information (for example, on out-of-state jobs, by using a computerized job bank) within the current employment-service structure, (3) additional mobile offices, (4) the seeking out and visiting of potential employees, and finally, (5) payment of job-seekers to train for a job and then subsidization of a move if necessary.

Estimates are available of the economic payoff from the last-named alternative. Table 1 shows that the economic payoff from subsidized migration to a new job can be large. For comparatively small cost, about $500 per family, people can be assisted in moving to places where jobs are more plentiful than in their home community. Studies indicate that the rate of back-migration after subsidized migration is frequently high, often reaching 60 percent during the first year and averaging 30 percent each year. The same studies indicate that adequate pre- and post-move counseling and financial help can substantially reduce the rate of back-migration.

TABLE 1. ESTIMATED ECONOMIC PAYOFF FROM SUBSIDIZED MIGRATION

Project	Relocatees	Rate of Return on Money Invested
	Number	Percent
Hartford	10	negative*
Minneapolis	46	8
Wisconsin–Michigan	255	20
Mississippi	255	24
North Carolina	485	33
Average of 67 projects		31

* Costs exceeded returns. The manpower situation shifted from excess supply to excess demand in the area during the period when the experiment in subsidized mobility was being organized. Considerable administrative expenses accrued, although few workers were relocated. This situation would be expected to occur occasionally in an expanded program, so it should be recognized as realistically portraying the merits of such efforts.

Source: Nelson and Tweeten (1973).

Frequently, vocational training needs to accompany these subsidized migration efforts.

Some foreign countries have had much more experience than the U.S. in subsidizing labor mobility. An interesting study by Jenness (1969) from Canadian experience improves on the methodolgy for evaluating mobility programs in several ways: (1) It accounts for changes in earnings for all family members, not just the male breadwinner; (2) it adjusts for each worker's personal history and characteristics; (3) it estimates the period over which the initial differential in earnings persists; and (4) it adjusts for the likelihood that some workers would have moved in the absence of a subsidy. Jenness (1969, pp. 111–12) computed a benefit-cost ratio of 3.9 for a favorable moving situation that would increase earnings by 50 percent. The Canadian experience indicates that an initial earnings increment of $1,000, or 20 percent, is more typical, thus implying a less favorable benefit-cost ratio for the typical case than that of 3.9 calculated by Jenness.

Improving Education and Training: Preparing People for Jobs

Education has a twofold effect on rural development: (1) It increases skills, and (2) it fosters attitudes consistent with socioeconomic progress. It broadens the outlook of people, enhances their motivation and aspirations for higher incomes and higher standards of living, and creates attitudes more nearly consistent with frictionless assimilation into a new environment.

A pilot project at McAlester, in the low-income Ozarks region of Oklahoma, was designed to generate an entrepreneurial spirit in a group of sixty-five adult males by formal means. The assumption of the study was that an attitude corresponding with McClelland's "need for achievement" can be taught, and that this will in turn lead to business activity that will create new jobs (cf. Tweeten, 1970, p. 427).

A follow-up study of McAlester trainees (and of a similar program conducted at Washington, D.C.) showed that each dollar spent on the program generated from $15 to $100 of new investment in just six months. The cost for each new job created by the program ranged from $100 to $300—a very favorable cost-effectiveness rating. The average increase in business profits during the first six months from each trainee ranged from a low estimate of $57 to a high of

$900. If these profits are maintained in perpetuity, the rate of return on training investment will range from 23 percent to 360 percent. These results are promising but tentative. Many years will be required to evaluate the full extent of the benefits of the program.

People-oriented development programs, such as education and training, have a high probability of success, because they tend to benefit the individual whether he leaves his home community or remains in it. Rates of return show the highest interest rate that could be paid on funds used for education (including foregone earnings) if one is just to break even on the investment. The rates of return shown in table 2 compare favorably with rates that could be earned on alternative investment opportunities. Social rates of return on investment (public and private) in the general education of U.S. white males are 18 percent for elementary schooling and 10 percent for secondary schooling and college. Rates are lower for nonwhite males and for females of all races. Private rates of return on only the investment made by the individual are, of course, higher than social rates of return.

TABLE 2. ESTIMATED RATES OF RETURN TO THE INDIVIDUAL (PRIVATE) AND SOCIETY (SOCIAL) FROM INVESTMENT IN SCHOOLING, WHITE MALES, 1959

| Schooling Level or Field of Study | United States | | Low-Income Rural Areas in South |
	Private Rate of Return	Social Rate of Return	Social Rate of Return
		Percent	
Elementary (grades 1–8)	155 (79)*	18 (10)*	26 (12)*
High School (grades 9–12)	16 (22)	10 (12)	11 (7)
College (grades 13–16)	14 (6)	10 (3)	2
Technical schooling (1960–1965 students, Okla. State Tech.)			
Average	15.6	8.6	
Automotive	5.8	1.4	
Commerce	10.6	4.4	
Diesel	21.4	14.4	
Drafting	23.2	17.4	
Electronics	21.5	15.1	
Refrigeration	17.7	12.0	

* Rates in parentheses are for nonwhite males.

Source: Tweeten (1970, pp. 137, 429); Shallah and Tweeten (1970).

Social rates of return on vocational training at Oklahoma State Tech are also shown in table 2. Rates tend to be at least as high as those from general education, according to a number of studies of the payoff from technical-vocational training reviewed by Shallah and Tweeten (1970) and by Hardin (1969).

Many states still rely to a considerable extent on local financing of schools. Efforts to improve human resources through education increase job mobility; this causes equity problems when the local expenditures for schooling accrue as benefits to another part of the state or to another state. Migration studies indicate that there is a large spill-in of benefits to states experiencing high net inmigration, such as California, from the education paid for, sometimes at great sacrifice, by residents of states with large net outmigration. Funding formulas need to be revised to compensate for net losses incurred by local communities and states, because the spill-out of their investment in schooling is not compensated for by the spill-in of capital embodied in inmigrants. Perhaps because taxpayers are reluctant to adequately support schools with large investment spillout and because of an inadequate resource base to tax, the general educational system is not adequately funded in many states. A new federal-state funding formula has been proposed, which takes into account (1) the desirable level of investment in schooling per student, (2) the net spillover of benefits among states, and (3) the ability of a state to finance education. Table 3 shows how this new formula for funding common schools would apply to Oklahoma.

Bringing Jobs to People

The above programs of improving human resources and bringing people to jobs have been underemphasized in the past. To many people, rural development means bringing jobs to rural areas. If this is the goal, it is still necessary to improve human resources: the documented heavy back-migration of rural people after an unfavorable experience with an urban job suggests that these people may also be unacceptable employees for a high-paying rural employer.

Nevertheless, there are many rural people who are able-bodied and underemployed but for whom outmigration is not the answer. For such persons, it is important to put teeth into programs to bring more jobs within commuting distance of rural residents. Current programs of technical assistance, low-interest loans, and public-

94

TABLE 3. ACTUAL AND OPTIMAL ELEMENTARY- AND SECONDARY-SCHOOL FUNDING PER STUDENT IN OKLAHOMA, SCHOOL YEAR 1959–1960

	Actual	Optimal
	Dollars	
Total educational expenditures		
Actual expenditures	465	
Amount needed to achieve an efficient or economically desirable level of education		766
State and local share		
Actual expenditure	429	
Optimal expenditure based on ability to pay ($436), less spill-outs ($76) from people migrating out of the state		360
Federal share		
Actual expenditure	36	
Expenditure to reach total optimal amount		406

facility grants are inadequate. And it seems unfair to ask depressed communities to subsidize the locating of industries. It has been suggested that firms be allowed a federal tax write-off on profits in proportion to the degree of underemployment in the rural areas in which they locate. A firm that locates in a designated growth center would write off from its corporate income taxes 1 percent of its plant investment for each 2 percent of underemployment in the economic-development district. In other words, if underemployment is 30 percent in the district, then the firm can deduct from its corporate federal income tax 15 percent of its investment in plant and equipment. This program would only be available to firms that locate where underployment exceeds, let us say, 20 percent.

Based on the most comprehensive data available, Singer (1972, p. 236) estimated that providing jobs through tax incentives for location of industry would entail a public subsidy (foregone taxes) of $8,000 to $17,000 per job created. This cost-per-job-created is within the bounds of an independent estimate by Tweeten (1970, p. 414), based on past efforts of the Economic Development Administration, that from $5,400 to $27,000 would be required to create a new job. The latter estimate assumes, perhaps unfairly, that all administrative costs of EDA should be charged to job creation.[4] Sazama (1970) has estimated that there would be favorable benefit-cost ratios for state loans, although other studies suggest that these programs are not effective in attracting industry (cf. Tweeten, 1970, p. 446).

Subsidized Private Employment

Job Opportunities in the Business Sector (JOBS), a program in which private industry is paid by the government to train and hire the disadvantaged, appears to be very cost-effective, creating a "permanent" new job for under $3,000 of direct federal funds per disadvantaged worker ("Zero Quota," 1970, p. 93). The retention rate in the JOBS program is between one-half and two-thirds. The JOBS program has two components—one in which industry has considerable choice in selecting trainees whom it trains and hires at no direct cost to the government, and another in which the firm has little choice in selecting trainees but is paid to train and employ them.

> One of the most important discouraging factors is that the contracted portion is very small. There has not been a breakthrough in getting business to take contracts for on-the-job training—contracts which make them feel obligated to take the kind of person supplied. Most of the businesses which have joined the program have gone into the free portion of the program where they can select their own trainees. They have been reluctant to take what one of the officials in the National Alliance of Businessmen called the "basket case." The indication, therefore, is that people selected for training are not from the hard-core or "basket case" group. (Levine, 1969, p. 179.)

Public training-employment programs may fare little better with this hard-core group. It is necessary to recognize that there are seemingly able-bodied workers who, for lack of initiative or aptitude, are unable to earn a socially acceptable wage, even after extensive training and subsidized employment, and for whom a simple transfer payment is the most cost-effective way to raise their incomes to an acceptable level.

Public Employment

Two recent programs, Operation Mainstream and New Careers, as well as New Deal programs of the 1930s, give some background for predicting the consequences of a large-scale effort by the government to assume the role of employer of last resort.

The Public Service Careers Program is designed to provide jobs in the public sector in a manner parallel to the JOBS program in the private sector, and it may provide jobs for 11 million disadvantaged persons by 1975 (U.S. Department of Labor, 1970, p. 73). The program, of which New Careers is one component, has not been in operation long enough to evaluate.

The Family Assistance Plan or related programs that require employment (or training) on the part of welfare recipients will increase the demand for employment opportunities, even in make-work projects for those who cannot obtain employment under competitive conditions. Levine (1969, p. 182) gives one view of the group of persons to be served and the type of work performed under public-service employment.

> These are people who are not now being recruited for manpower programs or who are not succeeding in these programs, but who might be capable of working. In 1965, on the basis of reports done for the Office of Economic Opportunity, the National Commission on Technology, Automation, and Economic Progress talked of five to six million jobs needed for poor people. This number may be far too high for the program I am outlining—it is an estimate of the needs of the public sector for all sorts of people, not just the residual poor who cannot make it elsewhere—but the true number is still likely to be substantial.
>
> What kind of jobs are we talking about in a public employment program? We are not talking about leaf-raking because it has a bad name, but we are talking about manual labor, of outdoor maintenance, including perhaps even the redistribution of arborial debris! We are talking perhaps about ditch-digging . . . the separation of sewers from other kinds of drainage lines, etc. We may be talking about work in the post office—which could hardly be done worse! We are not talking about doctor's aides and teacher's aides. (Levine, 1969, p. 182.)

The success of the program depends on (1) the contribution to real output; (2) the training, attitudes, and discipline acquired that would bring people up to satisfactory employability levels for competitive employment; and (3) the success in moving people from "make-work" public employment to competitive employment in a reasonable period of time, say eighteen months.

The wage should be somewhat above the level of income that

would be provided by public-assistance grants and below the wages available under competitive employment—hence, approximately $1.50 to $2.00 per hour. The wage should not be so high that workers would be bid away from more productive private employment.

Private industry is unlikely to tolerate government-run industry that competes directly with its own products. Furthermore, the candidates for public employment are likely to be the hard-core disadvantaged who, because of low aptitude, unreliability, or low initiative, are unable or unwilling to benefit from manpower training or competitive employment. Pooling these people together in public employment could cause them to reinforce one anothers' deficiencies; and working in dead-end jobs on make-work projects could accentuate their anomie. A large program of this type would surely develop an unfavorable public image. Perhaps this program should not only be an employer of last resort, but also a program of last resort.

Yet many people are optimistic about the program, and the public cost of raising income levels by it compare favorably to the public cost of raising income of the able-bodied through various negative-income-tax and other public-assistance programs. Pohlman (1970, p. 17) computed its benefit-cost ratios under specific assumptions concerning length of employment and productivity and concluded that

> in terms of the figures developed in this study, the normative implications are quite clear: If the government adopts a guaranteed annual income concept or sets minimum welfare standards, it will pay to develop as many job opportunities as possible. This is already the case in the industrial states which have more adequate welfare programs. Even when the only benefits considered are the reduced welfare expenditures, the investment in job opportunities is a sound one. When other benefits are considered, job creation becomes even more attractive.

Direct Grants

Public assistance in the forms of transfer payments ordinarily does not make federal funds go far toward raising incomes except for the nonsalvageable poor. But there are many instances in which transfer payments are more cost-effective than other programs. For many nonsalvageable poor, including the aged, the disabled, and mothers with preschool children, substantial funds may be spent on training for jobs in order to create future earnings which never materialize. In other instances, direct grants are necessary in order to maintain income until programs, such as family planning, that rank higher in long-term cost-effectiveness have had time to exert an influence. In other instances, direct grants may serve nonquantifiable humanitarian ends and may help to avoid riots.

There are several forms of "direct payments": (1) payments in services or goods, such as food donations; (2) cash grants, such as Aid to Families with Dependent Children; (3) partial grants, such as unemployment, retirement, disability, and medical compensation, in which the government and the private sector or individuals share the cost of the program; and (4) a negative income tax. Some of these are more cost-effective than others.

It can be shown in theory that welfare payments in cash rather than in an equivalent dollar volume of specific goods or services places the individual on a higher indifference (satisfaction) curve. The case for payment in kind is that society knows better than the individual what is good for him. The public perhaps is willing to provide more welfare funds if it has some say about how funds are spent by the poor. Tying welfare payments to education or to performance of work makes payments go farther to raise income, but it may give payments only to the particular "poor" who need assistance the least. There are many poor people who lack the capacities not only to earn a socially acceptable income but even to qualify for welfare grants by the most token of performance standards. For these, there are few alternatives to transfer payments.

Aid to Families with Dependent Children (AFDC) is the fastest growing and most controversial of the public-assistance programs. A 1961 amendment to the Social Security Act permitted families with an employable parent to receive federally supported assistance under the AFDC-UP program. As of 1970, only half of the states had adopted the program. Also work incentives were built into the AFDC program by 1967 amendments, which required that, beginning no later than July 1969, all states must disregard the first $30 of monthly earnings and one-third of all earnings above that amount in computing a family's AFDC allowance (U.S. Department of Labor, 1970, p. 151). Some success in moving welfare recipients to jobs and off welfare roles is apparent: during fiscal

LEWIS AND CLARK COLLEGE LIBRARY
PORTLAND, OREGON 97219

1969, welfare recipients enrolled in work and training programs administered by the Department of Labor numbered approximately 180,000, plus 100,000 youth from welfare families in the Neighborhood Youth Corps summer program. Based on a sample of 12,000 who completed Manpower Development Training Administration (MDTA) programs in fiscal 1967, an estimated 59 percent of the men and 62 percent of the women formerly on assistance obtained employment after training, compared to 75 percent of *all* men and 69 percent of *all* women who completed MDTA courses in 1967. Hourly earnings average $1.86 after training for former welfare recipients, only 10 cents per hour below the average for all MDTA graduates. The record appears promising but needs more careful economic evaluation.

The Family Assistance Plan

For adequate levels of living in the rural areas, welfare reforms are needed that would include the working poor, reduce the indignity of the means test, cut wasteful administrative apparatus, include built-in incentives for work and for family unity, reduce variation in payment rates and eligibility requirements among states, and reach more than the one-half of the poor receiving assistance in 1971. By providing uniform national norms of eligibility and by assuming a larger share of the cost of welfare (and education), the federal government would appear to be employing more equitable ways of "revenue-sharing" than by basing revenue-sharing on population or past federal aid. Many such improvements are included in the Family Assistance Plan; but many of these reforms have already been made in the AFDC program, which would be replaced by FAP.

To be eligible for FAP, able-bodied family members would have to accept available employment or training. Mothers with children under six years of age would be exempt from this rule, but many would be freed for employment by the day-care centers for children that would be established under the program.

Still, we should hold no illusions about the effect of FAP. Since less than 10 percent of persons on welfare are potentially employable, built-in work incentives would do little to increase employment for families now receiving welfare. And FAP would double the number (12 million in 1971) of persons receiving welfare. The additional millions would include many working poor. Many of these persons would work less. Hence, FAP would probably reduce national employment and output and would probably increase welfare costs. As a percentage of the gross national product, the real cost would be small and, in the minds of many, a small price to pay for a more equitable distribution of income.

An estimated 262,000 farm-operator and 232,000 farm-laborer families would be eligible for FAP in 1971. FAP plus food stamps would increase assistance nearly $1 billion to *farm* families over current welfare programs, and two-thirds of the gain would be in the South. Net gains to *rural* families would be nearly $3 billion, or roughly half the net gain to all U.S. families from FAP and food stamps. About four times as many U.S. rural families would be eligible for FAP benefits as would be eligible for benefits under the current AFDC or AFDC-UP programs in 1971.

In 1971 the gap between the poverty threshold and the income that poor families were receiving from all sources was about $8 billion. The proposed Family Assistance Plan plus the food stamp bonus would cut this poverty gap approximately in half.

A direct grant of the difference between current income and the poverty threshold would close the gap for $8 billion. A family assistance plan or a plan of the negative-income-tax type would require considerably more than $8 billion to close the gap, because many funds would go to the nonpoor. Thus a flat grant would be more cost-effective in eliminating poverty in the short run, but the work-incentive effects of a negative-income-tax plan might lead to greater effectiveness for it in the long run.

Farm Income Support Programs

Farm-commodity and land-retirement programs constitute the single most massive government effort to support rural incomes; they have entailed costs to the treasury of over $4 billion annually in recent years. It is well that such programs be included in systems planning for rural development.

Government payments associated with commodity programs are slightly less concentrated among large producers than are farm receipts. Estimates for 1965 indicate that in the absence of commodity programs, income of units with farm sales of $40,000 and over would fall $14,149 on the average, while income of units with farm sales of under $2,500 would fall $281 on the average (Tweeten and Schreiner, 1970, p. 54).

Data show that government programs for acreage diversion in the 1960s added $1.50 on the average to net farm income per government dollar spent (cf. Tweeten, 1970, chap. 11). Diversion programs have a "double-barreled" effect on farm income: The farmer receives a direct payment for participating in the program, plus indirect income as reduced production generates higher receipts through an inelastic demand. Current programs have not made government funds go as far as they could go to raise farm income, because emphasis has been placed on direct payments rather than on diverting production except in the feed-grain program.

Table 4 contains estimates of the cost-effectiveness of a long-term land-retirement program administered to remove as much production as possible per government dollar spent. The estimates assume that farmers would place land in the program if it pays to do so, a $2 payment is paid by the government per diverted acre for conservation practices, and land retirement is limited in any one county to no more than 30 percent of the cropland. The normative estimates of the value of production retired per dollar of program cost to the government are in line with actual performance of past

TABLE 4. ESTIMATED COST-EFFECTIVENESS OF LONG-TERM LAND RETIREMENT, BASED ON 1964–1966 PRICES

Acres Retired Nationally in Millions	Cumulative Government Cost in Millions of Dollars	Cumulative Value of Diverted Production in Millions of Dollars	Average Value of Production Retired per Dollar of Government Cost
10	105.0	508.2	4.84
20	348.9	1,078.1	3.09
30	569.4	1,474.8	2.59
40	842.7	1,938.3	2.30
50	1,215.9	2,541.2	2.09
60	1,690.7	3,296.8	1.95
70	2,062.9	3,857.6	1.87
80	2,554.4	4,597.9	1.80

* Because more production is diverted per dollar of program cost on marginal land, the first 10 million acres diverts less production but at lower government cost per unit of production than the last 10 million acres in table 4. See Tweeten (1970, chap. 11) for a thorough analysis of the relationship between cost-effectiveness and productivity of land.

Source: Zepp and Sharples (1970).

long-term land-retirement programs and would provide a useful schedule for interpolating the impact of alternative levels of voluntary production-control programs in the systems model. The systems estimates would probably show that land retirement is not a cost-effective means to raise incomes of poor rural people, but may be one cost-effective means to raise incomes of a rural region in the aggregate.

The contribution to farm income is larger than the value of production diverted, in part because the macro effects on farm receipts are not shown in table 4. In systems planning for any one region, the effects for that region could be calculated under the assumption that the program would be available to farmers in the entire nation, with macro and micro impacts prorated accordingly.

SUMMARY AND CONCLUSIONS

Improvements have been made in public programs to promote the development of and to improve living standards in rural areas. Yet these programs remain fragmented, overlapping, and inadequate, and they are frequently inefficient in reaching the desired development goals. The premise of this paper is that it is time to move from program-planning to plan-programming. This paper outlines the rudiments of a comprehensive, systems-programming approach to rural-development planning. Ideally, the approach (1) accounts for interactions among policies, (2) explicitly recognizes development targets, (3) shows trade-offs between targets such as efficiency and equity, and (4) measures the total public investment needed to reach development targets efficiently. A basic conflict exists between goals of efficiency (for example, maximum income per public dollar spent) and equity (for example, favorable distribution of benefits). Unmitigated pursuit of efficiency leads to public programs that by-pass the poor. Thus it is necessary to constrain systems solutions to meet targets such as reducing the incidence of poverty.

The coefficients in the systems-programming approach presented in this paper should reflect efficient development technology for any given program. Among other considerations, this requires coefficients for optimal-size growth centers, which provide public services at low cost per capita. Studies of economies of city size indicate that cities of 20,000 to 750,000 fulfill these requirements.

103

However, economic viability measured by ability to provide steady growth in jobs ordinarily requires growth centers larger than 20,000 population.

This paper outlines a basic model for comprehensive systems planning of rural development, but it does not contain empirical estimates from the model. The paper reports results of a number of studies of individual programs, which provide cost-effectiveness coefficients that could be a foundation for a comprehensive model.

The estimates of cost-effectiveness presented for individual programs suggest tentative priorities for an overall rural-development strategy. National full-employment and family-planning programs rank high in cost-effectiveness for use of public funds to improve the well-being of rural people. Adequate provision of family-planning services at public expense to assist the poor in having only the number of children that they desire would appear to deserve high priority in a rural-development program.

Approximate estimates of the efficiency of public monies in creating new employment opportunities are summarized in table 5. All of the programs assume a reasonably adequate level of skill training and general education and no excessive national unemployment—thus education and national monetary policies are not included in the priorities. The table shows estimated direct public expense for creating a permanent job for residents of rural areas. It appears that public employment, which many people recommend

TABLE 5. PUBLIC COST FOR CREATING A NEW JOB FOR RURAL WORKERS
IN 1972 BY ALTERNATIVE PROGRAMS

	Dollars
Public employment ($6,000 per year for 10 years with 40 percent productivity)*	36,000
Industry location through tax write-offs	12,000
JOBS program ($3,000 per job, one-half retention rate; including administrative costs)	6,000
Subsidized migration ($500 direct payment plus $500 for administration and counseling; one-third retention rate)	3,000

* The Value of the marginal product is assumed generously to be $2,400 per year and is deducted from the annual cost to the public. Future costs are not discounted to the present.
Source: Updated estimates based on studies cited in text.

as the solution to problems of underemployment in depressed areas, is an expensive way to create new jobs. The net cost, of course, depends on several factors, including the productivity of the workers involved in the program. If the workers are not productively employed, the cost is prohibitive. On the other hand, the JOBS program, which utilizes federal subsidies to private firms that train and hire the disadvantaged, requires a direct public outlay of only $6,000 per permanent job created. The JOBS program perhaps has limited viability in many rural areas, because there simply are not enough jobs available with private firms; but the program is a way of focusing jobs directly on disadvantaged workers, and it warrants use wherever possible.

Table 5 indicates that moving people to jobs can be more cost-effective than bringing jobs to people. Subsidized loan programs to bring industry and jobs to people are about as cost-effective as tax write-offs when operated at the same level of intensity. The fact that some past loan programs appear to have been more cost-effective partly reflects the fact that they operated at low levels of intensity. Areas that experience a large net outmigration should be compensated for their investment loss in the form of human capital embodied in outmigrants.

Many less mobile rural people are best served by bringing jobs within commuting distance. Programs such as a tax write-off to a locating industry are needed to bring jobs to people. For the disadvantaged but able-bodied workers in rural areas, it may be necessary to combine the two approaches of bringing jobs to people and people to jobs—by paying firms first to locate in viable rural centers, then to hire the disadvantaged.

And finally, for those people who cannot obtain adequate employment because of old age, disabilities, or other valid reasons, improvement in the welfare program—a plan of the negative-income-tax type in conjunction with the food stamps, family health insurance, and housing programs—would go a long way toward meeting these requirements. For the most disadvantaged, public-assistance transfer payments are more cost-effective than the programs in table 5, which are designed for able-bodied persons.

This paper is Journal Article 2253 of the Agricultural Experiment Station, Oklahoma State University, Stillwater, Oklahoma. Research reported herein was supported by the Agricultural Experiment Station and the National Science Foundation. The comments of Dean Schreiner, Gerald Doeksen, and George Brinkman were much appreciated by the author.

NOTES

1. This figure includes outlays for agriculture and rural development, natural resources, commerce and transportation, community development and housing, health, education, and manpower, but it excludes Social Security.

2. One "law" of public programs is that their benefits tend to be distributed regressively among those eligible for the program (Tweeten, 1970, p. 417).

3. Considerable data are available on characteristics of the populalation. Useful sources of data include the 1966 and 1967 Survey of Economic Opportunity (SEO) based on a sample of 30,000 households. The one-in-one-hundred sample from the 1970 U.S. Census of Population provides substantial additional detail. Considerable data have been assembled by the Urban Institute for a micro-simulation study of the impact of income-maintenance programs (Peabody and Caldwell, 1970). Other sources of data include personal interview surveys made in major poverty areas, which are useful if the system under analysis coincides with the survey regions.

4. These estimates for EDA are based on capital requirements of $20,000 per worker, which are higher than for nonmetropolitan industry in general but are not out of line for high-paying, progressive industries. These and other estimates used in this study do not consider the employment added directly in the form of personnel hired to administer the particular program.

REFERENCES

Bertalanffy, Ludwig von. "An Outline of General Systems Theory," *British Journal of the Philosophy of Science*, vol. 1 (1951), pp. 134–65.

Bogue, Donald J. "Acceptance of a Family Planning Program by the Rural Poor: Summary of an Experiment in Alabama." Chap. 22 in President's National Advisory Commission on Rural Poverty, *Rural Poverty in the United States*. Washington, D.C.: U.S. Government Printing Office, May 1968.

Coffey, Joseph. "Rural Manpower." 1971 National Agricultural Outlook Conference. Washington, D.C.: U.S. Department of Agriculture, 1971.

Greenberg, David, and Kosters, Marvin. "Labor Incentive Effects under a Negative Income Tax: Some Empirical Results." Santa Monica, Calif.: Rand Corp., 1970.

Hamilton, H. R., et al. *Systems Simulation for Regional Analysis: An Application to River-Basin Planning*. Cambridge, Mass.: M.I.T. Press, 1969.

Hardin, Einer. "Benefit-Cost Analysis of Occupational Training Programs: A Comparison of Recent Studies." Pp. 97–118 in G. G. Somers and W. D. Wood, ed., *Cost-Benefit Analysis of Manpower Policies*. Kingston, Ont.: Industrial Relations Center, Queens University, 1969.

Hathaway, Dale E., and Perkins, Brian E. "Occupational Mobility and Migration from Agriculture." Chap. 13 in President's National Advisory Commission on Rural Poverty, *Rural Poverty in the United States*. Washington, D.C.: U.S. Government Printing Office, May 1968.

Hines, Fred, and Tweeten, Luther. "Optimal Regional Funding of Elementary and Secondary Schooling." Agricultural Experiment Station Report P-669. Stillwater, Okla.: Oklahoma State University, 1972.

Jaffe, Frederick S. "Family Planning and Rural Poverty: An Approach to Programing of Services." Chap. 21 in President's National Advisory Commission on Rural Poverty, *Rural Poverty in the United States*. Washington, D.C.: U.S. Government Printing Office, May 1968.

Jenness, Robert. "Manpower Mobility Programs." Pp. 184–220 in G. G. Somers and W. D. Wood, eds., *Cost-Benefit Analysis of Manpower Policies*. Kingston, Ont., Industrial Relations Center, Queens University, 1969.

Kershaw, Joseph, and Courant, Paul. *Government against Poverty*. Chicago: Markham Publishing Co., 1970.

Klindt, Thomas, and Braschler, Curtis. "Costs, Revenues and Simulated Consolidation of Selected Missouri Counties." Missouri Agricultural Experiment Station Research Bulletin 949. Columbia, Mo., March 1969.

Levine, Robert. "Manpower Programs in the War on Poverty." Pp. 170–83 in G. G. Somers and W. D. Wood, eds., *Cost-Benefit Analysis of Manpower Policies*. Kingston, Ont.: Industrial Relations Center, Queens University, 1969.

Lu, Y. C.; Horne, James; and Tweeten, Luther. "Farming Opportunities for Farm Youth in Oklahoma and the United States." Oklahoma Agricultural Experiment Station Bulletin B-683. Stillwater, Okla., September 1970.

McLoughlin, J. Brian. *Urban and Regional Planning: A Systems Approach*. New York: Frederick A. Praeger, 1969.

Madden, J. Patrick. "Poverty by Color and Residence," *American Journal of Agricultural Economics*, vol. 50 (1968), pp. 1399–1412.

Morris, Douglas, and Tweeten, Luther. "The Cost of Controlling Crime: A Study in Economies of City Life [Size]," *Annals of Regional Science*, vol. 5, no. 1 (June 1971), pp. 33–49.

Nelson, James, and Tweeten, Luther. "Subsidized Labor Mobility," *Annals of Regional Science*, vol. 6 (1973).

Peabody, Gerald, and Caldwell, Steven. "Dynamic Microsimulation of the Impact of Income Maintenance Programs." Washington, D.C.: The Urban Institute, 1970.

Pohlman, Jerry. "A Cost-Benefit Analysis of Transfer Payments:

Job Creation vs. Welfare." Mimeographed. Buffalo, N.Y.: Department of Industrial Relations, State University of New York, 1970.

Sazama, Gerald. "A Benefit-Cost Analysis of a Regional Development Incentive: State Loans," *Journal of Regional Science*, vol. 10 (1970), pp. 385–96.

Shallah, Salim, and Tweeten, Luther. "Economic Returns to Technical Education." Oklahoma Agricultural Experiment Station Bulletin B-685. Stillwater, Okla., October 1970.

Singer, Neil. "Federal Tax Incentives for Regional Growth," *Southern Economic Journal*, vol. 38 (1971), pp. 230–37.

Tweeten, Luther. *Foundations of Farm Policy*. Lincoln, Nebr.: University of Nebraska Press, 1970.

———, and Schreiner, Dean. "Economic Impact of Public Policy."
Chap. 3 in Center for Agricultural and Economic Development, *Benefits and Burdens of Rural Development*. Ames, Iowa.: Iowa State University Press, 1970.

U.S. Department of Agriculture, Economic Research Service. Unpublished worksheets of Glenn Zepp and Jerry Sharples. Washington, D.C., 1970.

U.S. Department of Commerce. *Statistical Abstract of the United States*. Washington, D.C.: U.S. Government Printing Office, 1970.

U.S. Department of Labor. "Manpower Report of the President." Washington, D.C.: U.S. Government Printing Office, 1970.

U.S. Senate. Committee on Finance. "The Family Assistance Act of 1970," H.R. 16311, 91st Congress, 2d sess. Washington, D.C.: U.S. Government Printing Office, June 1970.

"Zero Quota," *Time*, 6 April 1970, p. 93.

108

USE OF NATURAL RESOURCES IN COMMUNITY DEVELOPMENT

EMERY N. CASTLE / Oregon State University

Some of the resources that a community may utilize for its development are the natural resources located around the community. These resources include land, water, air, minerals, and so forth, and such less visible resources as "open spaces" and "pleasant climates." Natural resources may be utilized by communities in a great variety of ways. Often natural resources directly provide employment through mining, petroleum extraction, and farming on agricultural land. Natural resources may also contribute to economic employment as inputs into production, for example, water for commercial manufacturing, transportation, and agricultural irrigation, and land for business locations. Recreational uses of lakes and reservoirs, hunting lands, and parks contribute to the satisfaction of community living; they also provide service jobs for tourists and vacationers. Even residential areas are dependent on the wise use of natural resources to provide safe, pleasant-looking neighborhoods.

Questions have arisen periodically during the past decade as to the implications of the use of natural resources in the development of rural communities and to the mutual relationship of community development and resource economics. This paper will attempt initially to summarize the relationship between community development and resource economics and then will devote major attention to some implications of the use of natural resources in community development.

Naturally, all communities are not endowed with equal natural resources, nor can they utilize their resources in the same manner. Communities in the Pacific Northwest, for example, often have access to abundant supplies of water, which is not available to the same extent in the Great Plains; whereas communities in the Plains have abundant supplies of open land, which is not found on the East Coast. Furthermore, climatic conditions may affect the use of natural resources and may influence the location and type of economic activity found in a particular area. Two studies are presented in this paper to illustrate the effect on a community's development alternatives of its comparative advantage in natural resources and the risk and uncertainty from natural hazards and climatic conditions. A third study illustrates the implications of natural-resource-development projects on income distribution. This third study demonstrates how resource-development projects such as water reservoirs, dams, and parks often represent transfers of income from the U.S. as a whole (which pays for the project) to the region of the project, where most of the benefits occur.

COMMUNITY DEVELOPMENT AND NATURAL-RESOURCE ECONOMICS

Most definitions of community development refer to it as a process involving group decisions and group action where there is (are) some common objective(s) or target(s) sought by the people constituting the community. In this process, people from many disciplines, including economists specializing in natural-resource economics, can participate and provide useful assistance. The term resource economics, in contrast, describes a body of knowledge within a particular discipline and relates to the economic use of natural resources.

The relationship between resource economics and community development takes on more meaning when one considers the strong interdependence of all elements in the process of community development. These elements include the human, natural, and capital rsources that are necessary to provide a viable community (in the group sense) and to provide satisfactory work and living opportunities for the individual members. By considering the democratic ethic that those who are affected by a decision are relevant to the making of that decision, the role of the decision-maker is also introduced. Community development, therefore, includes the production and use of goods and resources, both public and private, together with the decisions of producers, consumers, and all others directly or indirectly affected. These elements in community development are summarized below. The use of natural resources may be directed by both individual and group decision-making units and may facilitate community development through the production of both public and private goods.

I. Decision-units
 A. Individual
  1. Firms
  2. Households
 B. Groups
  1. City
  2. County
  3. Other

II. Resources
 A. Human

 B. Natural

 C. Capital Stock

III. Goods
 A. Goods
  Produced by
  Public Sector
 B. Goods
  Produced by
  Private Sector

The production of goods in the public sector from natural resources is the result of group decisions and choices about their use and development. Consequently, natural resources may be major components of public resources, such as parks, recreational facilities, and public water, as well as being used for private production and consumption. Many aspects of public-sector goods, however, are poorly understood and difficult to allocate throughout our economy. Ordinarily, the community is considered in the economic sense as a system of jobs, markets, and the geographic trade areas that function around it. By this approach we are using the system of markets that evolved to supply private goods to the community. The decision unit for public goods, on the other hand, may be very different, especially for those that are not considered market goods.

Many attributes of our natural environment, such as recreation and environmental quality, are not market goods in the private sense and consequently are not at this time within the present calculus of our economic systems. While our technology may have been successful in reducing the economic importance of such market commodities as agricultural land (through substitution of higher-yielding varieties, fertilizer, and so forth), some nonmarket attributes of natural resources may well have become relatively more scarce—for example, "open spaces" or "clean air." The provision and protection of these attributes becomes a part of the economics of public goods and is one of the contributions that resource economics can make.

NATURAL RESOURCES AND THE ECONOMIC CHOICE OF COMMUNITIES

Comparative Advantage in the Use of Natural Resources

By definition, no two communities can be identical with respect to their resources. Consequently, the alternatives for development through use of these resources is likely to be different for each community. The availability of a community's natural, capital, and human resources in comparison to other communities may do much to determine the community's comparative advantage for development and, in turn, the kinds of economic choices that the community may consider. At the local level, these choices are the decision alternatives that each individual community may utilize to foster its development. Policy prescriptions at the state or national level that do not take into account this uniqueness of communities with respect to resources probably will not be well accepted in this nation.

The impact of the uniqueness of resources on the range of choices open to a community can be illustrated by a case study from Oregon. A study has been made of the economics of water-quality issues stemming from the location of a pulp paper mill on Yaquina Bay.[1] In this example, the pulp mill utilizes the water flowing into the bay in their plant operation, for transportation, and as a depository for waste materials. Yaquina Bay is used for recreation and is the source of some commercial aquatic products, which are jeopardized by pollution from the pulp mill.

In the Yaquina Bay study, the direct and indirect benefits of the pulp mill, the effects of its pollution on recreation, and the cost of pollution control were examined to investigate the alternative choices open to the community and to the pulp mill. The variables are defined as:

R_P Direct benefits of recreation. These are the benefits that people get from utilizing the recreational facilities. These can be measured as the amount of money that people are willing to sacrifice rather than do without the recreational experience. This benefit would accrue to the community if recreationists reside in the community or if an admission charge is made to those who reside outside the community.

R_S Indirect benefits of recreation. These benefits consist mainly of the increases in net incomes of businesses serving those who engage in outdoor recreation.

P_P Direct benefits of the paper mill. The economic advantage of the Yaquina Bay location over an alternative location.

P_S Indirect benefits resulting from the operations of the paper mill.

C_P Cost of pollution control.

The relationships of the above variables in the case study are summarized by the following relationships:[2]

1. $P_P > C_P$
2. $P_P > (R_P + R_S)$
3. $C_P > (R_P + R_S)$

First, the primary benefit to the paper mill from locating at Yaquina Bay is greater than the cost of pollution control. Second, this direct benefit to the plant from its location here is also greater than the combined loss of direct and indirect recreational benefits caused by pollution from the plant. In other words, the primary gain to the plant resulting from this location is greater than the overall external loss from pollution. The third equation indicates that the cost of pollution control is also greater than the loss from pollution. Ignoring considerations of uncertainty and irreversibility, these relationships suggest that net social benefits could be derived from locating the plant at Yaquina Bay. Furthermore, it would be "economic" to suffer the diseconomy of pollution, rather than to impose pollution control to continue the benefits from recreation, because the cost of pollution control is greater than the loss of recreational benefits. Since the pulp mill would benefit at the expense of the recreational users, however, equity considerations would indicate that some type of compensation to the recreational users would be in order. If the plant paid the potential recreational users an amount that was greater than their benefits from recreation but less than the plant's cost of pollution control, both the recreation users and the plant would be better off.

The alternative choices open to the community in this example, however, are somewhat greater than national efficiency considerations would indicate. Because the cost of pollution control is less than the advantage of the location to the firm, pollution control can be imposed and will be accepted by the plant if the community wants to preserve the environment for future generations. (In the case study, pollution control has been imposed and accepted. It was imposed after the plant had been located, although the available evidence indicates that the location benefits were greater than the costs of pollution control.) In this example, it is possible for the community to have both this particular industry *and* preserve its recreational activity for future generations if it so desires, even though the costs of pollution control exceed present benefits from use of the bay for recreational purposes. Consequently, this case study illustrates the necessity of analyzing the use of natural resources within the uniqueness of each community's comparative advantage. Depending on the magnitude of the various costs and benefits to industrial plants, users of recreational services, home owners, and so forth, other communities may face considerably different choices.

Table 1 is presented to illustrate the institutional implications of a community's comparative advantage with respect to natural resources by showing some of the differences in choices that may exist with alternative economic conditions. These choices range from the Yaquina Bay case, where a community can have the industry and still impose pollution restrictions, to situations in which the community would be better off without the industry. The placement of a community within such a framework can give real insight into community-development options.

Risk and Uncertainty, Natural Hazards, and Economic Choice by Communities

A second factor influencing the economic choice of use of natural resources is the risk and uncertainty caused by natural hazards such as floods, droughts, windstorms, freezing, and so forth. A group of geographers stated recently: "A paradox is presented in man's apparently growing susceptibility to injury from natural hazards during a period of enlarged capacity to manipulate nature. . . . Nature retreats on every hand, and man, armed with a burgeoning

Table 1. Possible Outcomes in the Relationship of Economic Variables and Bargaining Implications

Situation 1	Relationship
$P_p > C_p$	The direct benefit of location to the paper mill is
$P_p > (R_p + R_s)$	greater than the cost of pollution control and the
$C_p > (R_p + R_s)$	location benefits are also greater than the loss of recreational benefits. Pollution-control costs are greater than the loss of recreational benefits. (The Yaquina Bay example.)

Bargaining Implications

The public district can decide if it wishes to use the locational advantage (P_p) to preserve the environmental quality (waste disposal or treatment) or to suffer the diseconomy—possibly working out some sort of compensation by the plant for the loss of recreational benefits. Preservation of environmental quality comes at a social cost of the excess of pollution-control expenses over recreational benefits.

Situation 2	Relationship
$P_p > C_p$	Same as situation 1, except that the cost of pollution
$P_p > (R_p + R_s)$	control is less than the recreational benefits.
$C_p < (R_p + R_s)$	

Bargaining Implications

The public district will wish to use part of P_p to preserve environmental quality, since C_p is less than the diseconomy $(R_1 + R_2)$.

Situation 3	Relationship
$P_p < C_p$	The indirect benefits from the plant location of P_s
$P_p < (R_p + R_s)$	must be considered in this situation, because direct
$(P_p + P_s) > C_p$	plant location benefits alone are less than the loss
$(P_p + P_s) > (R_p + R_s)$	of recreational benefits or the cost of pollution control. Total plant location benefits $(P_p + P_s)$ however are greater than either the loss of recreational benefits or the cost of pollution control.

Bargaining Implications

The community would be better off with the industry. Whether environmental quality is preserved or the diseconomy suffered would be similar to decisions outlined in situation 1. If environmental quality is preserved, cost-sharing with the industry will be necessary, since the direct benefits to the industry are less than the total costs of pollution control.

Situation 4	Relationship
$P_p < C_p$	Same as situation 3, except that total plant-location
$P_p < (R_p + R_s)$	benefits are less than the loss of recreational bene-
$(P_p + P_s) > C_p$	fits. The total plant-location benefits, however, are
$(P_p + P_s) < (R_p + R_s)$	greater than the costs of pollution control.

115

TABLE 1. *Continued*

Bargaining Implications

The community will be better off with the industry, but cost-sharing of waste disposal or treatment with the industry would be necessary. If waste disposal or treatment were not feasible, the community would be better off without the industry.

Situation 5	Relationship
$P_p < C_p$	Same as situation 3, except that the cost of pollu-
$P_p < (R_p + R_s)$	tion is greater than the total benefits of plant
$(P_p + P_s) < C_p$	location.
$(P_p + P_s) > (R_p + R_s)$	

Bargaining Implications

The community will be better off with the industry, since total plant-location benefits are greater than the loss of recreational benefits. However, since the cost of pollution control is greater than the total plant-location benefits, the community would be better off to suffer the diseconomy of pollution.

Situation 6	Relationship
$P_p < C_p$	Both the costs of pollution control and the loss of
$P_p < (R_p + R_s)$	recreational benefits from pollution are greater than
$(P_p + P_s) < C_p$	the total direct and indirect benefits of the plant
$(P_p + P_s) < (R_p + R_s)$	location.

Bargaining Implications

The community is better off without the industry.

technology, is asserting his ecological dominance yet more surely." Yet "mankind appears to be little nearer the conquest of nature in its more violent and extreme fluctuations. Rather, the magnitude of the impact of rare natural events upon society is increasing in terms of real property damage and loss of life, although there is verbal reluctance to accept these costs."[3] The thesis of this section is that variability in the response that is obtained from identical inputs of the human resource and capital over time because of climate and other natural phenomena has a considerable impact on the range of both individual and group choice.

Geographic areas may vary greatly with respect to the "cost" of incorrect choices caused by weather and natural hazards. The greater the variability with respect to natural phenomena, the greater the cost for the "extreme" event (such as a severe drought or flood). Individual adjustments to these extreme events will have impacts on the community. For example, a research study of geography and variations in agricultural income from natural hazards found that an inverse relationship existed in Kansas between (1) the earnings of male farmers and farm managers and (2) climatic "benevolence."[4] Farmers in the western Great Plains have typically adjusted to the costs of extreme economic events (low rainfall, strong hot winds, and so forth) by specializing and by increasing farm size. This has enabled the farmers who could make these adjustments to earn higher incomes, but many other farmers have gone out of business and left the Plains. As a result, there is little concentrated poverty in the Great Plains, but the effects of sparse populations are very pronounced.

Discovery of the types of institutional arrangements, economic activities, and technology that can mitigate the costs of the more extreme events would appear desirable from a normative standpoint. Increasing the range of choice, however, also increases the possibility of "wrong" choices. Those social devices that minimize the social and economic costs of adjustment will probably not be neutral with respect to the type of population that is attracted. For example, are the population characteristics the same for the Great Plains as for the Deep South or the eastern corn belt?

It appears safe to generalize with respect to three rudimentary propositions. (1) The cost or the penalty of a wrong decision must be taken into account in evaluating or predicting human adjustment. It is not enough to treat it as a negative reward and the sum of outcomes over time, as one severe mistake may permanently put a person out of business. (2) Human institutions, as well as natural hazards, affect these penalties. (3) The study of human adjustment to natural phenomena may provide insight into social phenomena necessary for the design of social institutions.

Because the relationships described in the preceding paragraphs are novel and have not been thoroughly researched, additional elaboration and development is appropriate. In areas where extreme natural events inflict a high economic cost on individuals, residents of a community will make some predictable adjustment if this high economic cost has been previously experienced or can be predicted with reasonable accuracy. For example, in the Great Plains, recurrent drought may be so severe as to force people to leave a community. Some of the social cost of this may even be

117

transferred to the remainder of the economy, as additional problems are caused from migration to other areas and large cities. Some of the cost, however, cannot be transferred and tends to be reflected in problems of providing social services for a sparse population. In this instance, however, the costs tend to be external to the individual farm, which increases its size to account for the risk of uncertainty. Of course, those individuals forced to leave a community may bear individual costs.

At the other extreme one can find the benign climate that does not force adjustment. Examples within the United States include those areas where natural conditions permit a highly diversified agriculture. Here, one often finds lower average farm incomes than in areas of more severe natural hazards. The reason is that survival is possible and costs of failure to adjust to changing economic conditions are more likely to be internalized within the individual firm. Social costs may be experienced, of course, because of low income, but these are more likely to remain within the community itself.

Recent research by Forrester suggests that the phenomena described above are not confined to rural communities and natural hazards.[5] He reports that the provision of low-income housing in urban areas may worsen the economic plight of urban residents. The reason is basically the same as the one given above—unemployed or low-income residents will take advantage of the low-income housing rather than make the economic adjustment of moving to other locations that offer the prospect of employment or higher income. The community-development implications become apparent. Adjustments to natural hazards may take the form of individual or group action. When the costs of the extreme event are high and fall largely on the individual, migration from the community will be a predictable adjustment. If the variance of the individual cost is low, the adjustment may be in lower income or underemployment. When a community attempts to cushion the shock of adjustment either to severe economic conditions or natural hazards by attempting to provide more benign or favorable conditions, the adjustment may be postponed, and the cost of the adjustment may be increased rather than being avoided. The incidence of the cost also will be changed from the individual to the community and society as a whole.

THE INTERFACE OF PUBLIC AND PRIVATE GOODS AND THE DISTRIBUTION OF INCOME FROM RESOURCE-DEVELOPMENT PROJECTS

It is a cliche to state that ours is a mixed economy. Yet, because it is a mixed economy, effective public group decisions will usually take into account probable reactions by the private sector. Or, to put the issue the other way around, whether a private action is permissible may be determined by its impact on the production and distribution of public goods, such as clean or pleasant views. Of central importance in this issue is the distribution of the costs and benefits of natural-resource development.

Numerous studies have been completed that analyze the public-private relationships that would be affected by a community decision. Many public decisions involving the interface of public and private goods relate to natural-resource management. Some examples are pollution from automobiles, a change in the allowable timber-cut or grazing on federally owned land, the effect of a change in the water quality of a large lake, or major reclamation projects.[6] In these examples, the distribution of the various benefits and trade-offs among the public and private units involved has obvious political implications. Identifying the people who are affected economically, and how much they are affected, by a given community economic-policy choice may help substantially in choosing among policy alternatives.

This can be illustrated further by some research on the economic consequences of transferring water from one region of the U.S. to another.[7] Even though this is a national and regional decision rather than one of a local community, the issues and the methodology are relevant to community-development decisions.

In this particular case example, the transfer of water from a relatively water-abundant region in the U.S. to a water-scarce region was undertaken to analyze the level and distribution of the benefits. Four general regions were studied. These were the region of origin (the Pacific Northwest), the region of transit (through which the water must be transferred), the region of destination (the Southwest), and the rest of the country. These regions are diagramed below.

In this water-transfer problem, it is assumed that 20 million acre-feet of water will be transferred annually from the region of

119

origin to the region of destination. The direct and indirect effects of the water transfer have been estimated for each of the four regions by calculating the benefits and the costs of the water-transfer project. The direct benefits are primarily represented by increased production, increased payments for labor, and increased supplies for

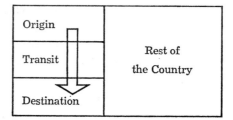

construction and maintenance in each region. The direct costs represent primarily the costs of water to the users, construction and maintenance expenditures, and tax expenditures. The indirect effects are multiplier effects resulting from increased or decreased economic activity in each region. Positive multiplier effects are indicated in the regions where new construction would occur and income would increase, while negative effects have been indicated where the regional economy would contract from a new outflow of funds. These cost and benefit calculations are given in table 2.

The above exercise is helpful in understanding a number of issues in political economy. In the example analyzed in table 2, at the interest rate assumed, the total benefits throughout the nation

TABLE 2. DISTRIBUTION OF BENEFITS AND COSTS OF A WATER-TRANSFER PROJECT FOR AN OVERALL U.S. BENEFIT-COST RATIO OF 1.0

Region	Net Direct Effects	Net Indirect Effects	Total Net Effect	Regional Benefit-Cost
	Dollars	Dollars	Dollars	Ratio
Entire Nation ..	0	0	0	1.0
Destination	+ 718,713,333	+ 777,893,333	+ 1,496,606,666	2.3
Origin	− 33,596,667	+ 41,839,999	+ 8,243,332	1.0+
Transfer	+ 71,023,333	+ 70,613,333	+ 141,636,666	1.5
Rest of Nation	− 756,139,999	− 890,346,665	− 1,646,486,664	No benefits but represents an income transfer

are just equal to the total costs, with no net social gains. The national economic-efficiency effects are therefore zero. From the standpoint of the four regions, however, the efficiency effects are far from neutral. Most of the benefits occur in the region of destination while most of the costs are borne by the remainder of the country. Consequently, this reclamation project represents a transfer of income from the large area of the United States physically unaffected by the water-development project to the region of destination by means of the transfer and development of natural resources.

Those economists who insist on adopting a national point of view in all of their analyses will fail to appreciate the economic motivation underlying many political positions. They will also fail to make their work relevant to those who concern themselves with decisions at a level other than that of the entire economy. Often, the regional and indirect effects of a project have greater significance on a micro level than the national and direct effects, particularly in determining political activity and power. It has long been recognized that the Chambers of Commerce in Western towns are more avid seekers of new reclamation projects than are farmers, because it is likely that the increased economic activity will greatly benefit the commercial interests. (Indirect benefits through multipliers.) When the prospective gains from a proposed public investment have been capitalized into property values, a potential political force of considerable strength has been created. The controversy and public outcry over the negative findings of the economists at the University of Arizona pertaining to the national efficiency of the Central Arizona Water Development Project is an illustration. (The psychological impact of the loss of prospective capital gains may be rather severe.) The costs, on the other hand, are spread over a great many people throughout the U.S., who are much less likely to organize as opposition. Consequently, most political activity comes from the minority, who stand to benefit the most, rather than from the majority, who must bear the cost.

The issue of multiple objectives emerges from such considerations. Much has been heard recently concerning the accomplishment of regional-development objectives by public investment in natural-resource development. It is obvious that traditional benefit-cost analysis is, at best, an incomplete guide for such decisions. The central issue becomes one of evaluating alternative means of accomplishing the regional-development objective. For example, in the case just analyzed, a principal economic effect of the hypothetical water transfer would be to transfer income to the area of water destination. Two questions immediately arise: (1) Is transferring income to this particular region a priority social objective? (2) If so, is this particular method of transferring income through resource development the most desirable means of accomplishing this objective?

NOTES

1. H. H. Stoevener, Joe B. Stevens, Howard F. Horton, Adam Sokolosky, Loys P. Parrish, and Emery N. Castle, "Multi-Disciplinary Study of Water Quality Relationship: A Case Study of Yaquina Bay, Oregon," Special Report 348 of Oregon Agricultural Experiment Station (February 1972).

2. In research that was done on this problem, numerical estimates have been made for all of the variables except the direct benefits of the paper mill, P_p, which appear to be greater than C_p, the cost of pollution control. The numerical estimates and the methods used to obtain them are not presented here, however, because relative magnitudes are all that are necessary to illustrate the economic choices that were available.

3. Ian Burton et al., "The Human Ecology of Extreme Geophysical Events," Working paper no. 1, 1968, an unpublished manuscript.

4. David W. Norman and Emery N. Castle, "Geography and Agricultural Income: An Additional Hypothesis," *Journal of Farm Eco-*

nomics, vol. 49, no. 3 (August 1967), pp. 571-83.

5. Jay W. Forrester, "Counterintuitive Behavior of Social Systems," *Technology Review*, vol. 73, no. 3 (January 1971).

6. D. F. Bromley et al., "Effects of Selected Changes in Federal Land Use on a Rural Economy," Station Bulletin 604 of the Oregon State University Agricultural Experiment Station (Corvallis, Oreg., 1968); Theodore G. Collin, "An Interindustry Analysis of the Effects of a New Industry on the Public and Private Sectors in Clatsop County, Oregon" (Master's thesis, Oregon State University, 1970); Stephen Reiling, "The Estimation of Regional Secondary Benefits Resulting from an Improvement in Water Quality of Upper Klamath Lake, Oregon: An Interindustry Approach" (Master's thesis, Oregon State University, 1971); H. H. Stoevener, "An Economic Evaluation of Water Pollution Control Alternatives: A Progress Report," Report no. 12 of the Committee on the Econom-

ics of Water Resource Development (1963), pp. 53–58; and H. H. Stoevener, "Water Use Relationships As Affected by Water Quality," in *New Horizons for Resources Research: Issues and Methodology*, Western Resources

Papers (Boulder, Colo.: University of Colorado Press, 1964).
7. Bruce R. Beattie et al., "Economic Consequences of Interbasin Water Transfer," Technical Bulletin 116 of Oregon State University Agricultural Experiment Station (Corvallis, Oreg.).

BIBLIOGRAPHY

Barnett, Harold J., and Morse, Chandler. *Scarcity and Growth: The Economics of Natural Resource Availability.* Baltimore, Md.: Resources for the Future, Inc., 1963.

Beattie, Bruce R.; Castle, Emery N.; Brown, William G.; and Griffin, Wade. "Economic Consequences of Interbasin Water Transfer." Technical Bulletin 116, Oregon State University Agricultural Experiment Station. Corvallis, Oreg.

Bromley, D. F.; Blanch, G. E.; and Stoevener, H. H. "Effects of Selected Changes in Federal Land Use on a Rural Economy. Station Bulletin 604, Oregon State University Experiment Station. Corvallis, Oreg., 1968.

Burton, Ian; Kates, Robert W.; and White, Gilbert F. "The Human Ecology of Extreme Geophysical Events." Working paper no. 1, 1968, an unpublished manuscript.

Castle, Emery N. "Economic and Administrative Problems of Water Pollution." A paper prepared for the American Association for the Advancement of Science, 27 December 1966.

———. "The Market Mechanism, Externalities, and Land Economics," *Journal of Farm Economics*, vol. 47, no. 3 (August 1965), pp. 542–56.

Ciriacy-Wantrup, Siegfried von. *Resource Conservation: Economics and Policies.* Berkeley, Calif.:

University of California Press, 1952.

Collin, Theodore G. "An Interindustry Analysis of the Effects of a New Industry on the Public and Private Sectors in Clatsop County, Oregon. Master's thesis, Oregon State University, 1970.

Forrester, Jay W. "Counterintuitive Behavior of Social Systems," *Technology Review*, vol. 73, no. 3 (January 1971).

Heady, Earl O. *Economics of Agricultural Production and Resource Use.* New York: Prentice-Hall, 1952.

Margenau, Henry. "What Is a Theory?" In S. R. Krupp, ed., *The Structure of Economic Science.* Englewood Cliffs, N.J.: Prentice-Hall, 1966.

Norman, David W., and Castle, Emery N. "Geography and Agricultural Income: An Additional Hypothesis," *Journal of Farm Economics*, vol. 49, no. 3 (August 1967), pp. 571–83.

Reiling, Stephen. "The Estimation of Regional Secondary Benefits Resulting from an Improvement in Water Quality of Upper Klamath Lake, Oregon: An Interindustry Approach. Master's thesis, Oregon State University, 1971.

Schultz, Theodore W. *The Economic Organization of Agriculture.* New York: McGraw-Hill, 1953.

Stoevener, H. H. "An Economic Evaluation of Water Pollution Control Alternatives: A Progress Report." Report no. 12, Committee on the Economics of Water Resource Development, 1963, pp. 53–58.

———. "Water Use Relationships As Affected by Water Quality." In *New Horizons for Resources Research: Issues and Methodology.* Western Resources Papers. Boul-der, Colo.: University of Colorado Press, 1964.

———; Stevens, Joe B.; Horton, Howard F.; Sokolosky, Adam; Parrish, Loys P.; and Castle, Emery N. "Multi-Disciplinary Study of Water Quality Relationship: A Case Study of Yaquina Bay, Oregon." Special Report 348, Oregon Agricultural Experiment Station. February 1972.

RURAL POVERTY AND URBAN GROWTH: AN ECONOMIC CRITIQUE OF ALTERNATIVE SPATIAL GROWTH PATTERNS

NILES M. HANSEN / University of Texas

Poverty is a major problem in the development of many rural areas. The fourth paper in this volume pointed out that there were 35.5 million people in poverty in 1970 in the U.S., with 12.1 million (nearly half) living in nonmetropolitan areas. Since nonmetropolitan areas contain only 31% of the total population, the incidence of poverty there is nearly 70% higher than in metropolitan areas. Poverty in nonmetropolitan areas is heavily concentrated among Negroes and whites in the Deep South and the Ozarks, primarily among whites in Appalachia and the Great Lakes area, among Mexican-Americans in the Southwest, and among Indians scattered throughout the central and western U.S. About 8.5 million of the total 12.1 million people in poverty in nonmetropolitan areas were white, 3.5 million black, and about 100,000–150,000 were Indians.

Increased urbanization and decreased opportunities for agricultural employment have made it difficult to close the gap between lagging rural areas with high incidences of poverty and the more economically advanced parts of the nation. The first section of this paper analyzes prospects for reducing rural poverty through investments in both rural and urban areas; it concentrates on intermediate-sized cities as growth centers relevant to migrants from rural areas. The second section analyzes investment in human resources as an alternative to subsidized public works and industrial-location incentives as the major developmental assistance within the areas of rural poverty. Both of these sections are primarily concerned with residents of impoverished or lagging rural areas, though the different problems of outmigration from rural areas where incomes and education levels are relatively high are also taken up. Finally, a number of future research needs related to these problems are indicated.

RURAL DEVELOPMENT VERSUS URBAN GROWTH

Although urbanization is apparently a necessary concomitant of economic development, the problem of poverty in lagging rural areas is often held to be a misfortune that should be alleviated by policies for the development of rural areas. Usually these policies involve a relatively heavy emphasis on subsidies to industry in the form of public-works projects and tax advantages. Attempts to justify these efforts are generally based on several arguments. One of the most popular is to appeal to the notion of rural-urban "balance," but it is rarely specified in concrete terms what this means. Frequent appeal also is made to the growth-center concept on the ground that concentration of investment in a relatively few centers in or near rural areas with growth potential results in the realization of external economics and beneficial spread effects to the growth centers' hinterlands.

Problems of Developing Lagging Rural Areas

Unfortunately, neither industrialization efforts in the areas themselves nor spread effects from investments in "growth centers" that have been the focus of federal policy have significantly improved economic conditions in lagging rural poverty areas. For example, an in-depth analysis of the Economic Development Administration's growth-center strategy, which has been directed toward small towns and cities, concludes that

> EDA's experience in funding projects in economic development centers has not yet proven that the growth center

126

strategy outlined in the Agency's legislation and clarified in EDA policy statements is workable. The Agency's approach to assisting distressed areas through projects in growth centers has resulted in minimal employment and service benefits to residents of depressed counties.[1]

Of course, there has been considerable growth in the past decade in nonmetropolitan counties that surround larger spontaneous growth centers, but these are usually larger metropolitan centers whose growth is not related to regional policy. Moreover, the nonmetropolitan growth resulting from the expansion of major urban fields has usually not taken place in poverty areas; growth has rather been accelerated in counties that were already experiencing growth. This has been especially apparent in the Upper Middle West (around such centers as Milwaukee, Madison, and Minneapolis–St. Paul) and in the South (around such centers as Atlanta, Nashville, Knoxville, Birmingham, Little Rock, Dallas, and Houston).

On the other hand, there has been considerable decentralization of manufacturing to rural areas in recent years. Whole regions of the South—for example, the Ozarks and the Tennessee Valley—have been particularly affected by this phenomenon. Unfortunately, the firms involved tend to be in slow-growing or declining industries; they also tend to be labor intensive (often employing mostly women) and tend to pay low wages. Moreover, the areas that have attracted firms of this type are overwhelmingly white in racial composition. In the long run the areas that have recently benefited from industrial decentralization may be able to upgrade the kinds of firms being attracted, but this would still leave many lagging rural areas with poor employment opportunities and low incomes per capita.

The poor record of efforts to solve rural poverty in the lagging areas themselves indicates that rural and small-city residents in these areas will probably have to move elsewhere to pull themselves out of poverty. Most of these people will need to migrate to urban centers for satisfactory employment, often to centers outside of the lagging areas. The migration from rural to urban areas, however, has often created social problems, which in turn have generated much of the support for the development of lagging rural areas. Advocates of rural development claim that every effort should be made to give everyone a job where he now lives, because migration from rural poverty areas to big cities results in greater social costs than the costs that would be involved in implementing their proposals. This raises two questions. First, are big cities (over 750,000) really too big? And second, are rural areas and small towns, on the one hand, and big cities, on the other, the only alternatives? Proponents of rural development are quite likely correct in saying that the big cities are too big and that they are undesirable destinations for rural migrants. The assumption that all cities face the plight of the big cities, however, is unjustified, as this ignores job opportunities and living conditions in intermediate-sized cities (200,000–750,000 population). These propositions are considered in more detail in the next section.

Problems of Big Cities and the Growth Prospects of Intermediate-sized Cities

Whether or not big cities in the United States are too big cannot be proven. The author has considered both sides of this issue elsewhere and has suggested that they probably are too big in terms of alternatives available to individuals and firms in intermediate-sized cities.[2] It may be that the difficulties of the big cities are not so much inherent in their size as in their structure, particularly where it is a question of a bifurcation between blacks in the central city and whites in the suburbs. Indeed, this position is widely held among the supporters of the big cities. In this event, there are two fundamental solutions to the problems of the cities: to break down the barriers imposed on the black population by discrimination and to pump more money into the cities to make them more habitable.

But these arguments are not convincing. In the first place, nations all over the world are finding that their big cities are too big, and an ever-increasing number of urban policies are aimed at checking their growth. While it is obvious that there are structural problems in American cities, this should not be an excuse for evading the difficulties of sheer size and density. Moreover, to the extent that we have structural problems, they would be easier to deal with if a migration policy would encourage migrants to locate in places other than the big cities. Finally, the argument that big cities can be saved by means of huge doses of federal investment is not in itself appealing. It is the same argument used by the proponents of rural areas and small towns to save many of them from natural death—

and no doubt eastern Kentucky, Southern Texas, and the Indian reservations *could* be made into very attractive places for people and industry if *enough* money were pumped in. The real question must be posed in terms of spatial opportunity cost: Are there better alternatives in other places? The big cities and the small towns and rural areas obviously need and will receive a great deal of public investment; but it does not seem wise to single them out for special favor, especially when a growth-center strategy based on inter-mediate-sized cities offers more opportunities in terms of existing external economies than do small towns and rural areas, and fewer diseconomies than do the big cities.

Without speaking of disadvantages, do the big cities have real economic advantages over intermediate-sized cities? The issue here is not one of optimum size but rather of the minimum size required to provide the range of services needed by people and firms and of the impact of size on growth potentials.

Brian Berry has found that above a population of 250,000 "the necessary conditions for self-sustaining growth seem satisfied," and he suggests that the greatest payoff in terms of increasing employment and reducing unemployment would be to use "the public treasury to enable centers close to this point to achieve self-sustaining growth" rather than to put resources into places much smaller than this maximum.[3] Similarly, Wilbur Thompson proposes that there is an urban size ratchet and that when the population growth of an urban area reaches a critical size of around 250,000, it appears that "structural characteristics, such as industrial diversification, political power, huge fixed investments, a rich local market, and a steady supply of industrial leadership may almost ensure its continued growth and fully ensure against absolute decline—may, in fact, effect irreversible aggregate growth."[4]

Australian data indicate that most of the advantages of a city of 500,000 probably also are found in a city of 200,000, but that if a city gets much beyond the 500,000 level, external diseconomies are likely to begin to outweigh the concomitant economies. On the basis of Australian experience, Neutze suggests that many firms will maximize their profits in centers with populations between 200,000 and 1 million.[5] In an earlier study Colin Clark examined structural differences in American, Canadian, and Australian cities of different sizes. He concluded that a city of about 200,000 provides practically all important services and that a city is "full grown" with respect to manufacturing at a population level of around 500,000.[6]

The data that we have with respect to the provision of public services indicate that both small towns and big cities fare worse than intermediate-sized cities. For example, Werner Hirsch estimates that the greatest economies of scale occur in cities in the 50,000 to 100,000 range, whereas the Royal Commission on Local Government in Greater London found the range to be from 100,000 to 250,000.[7] Gordon Cameron finds a "U-shaped" infrastructure cost curve, with the minimum cost lying between somewhat less than 300,000 and somewhat more than 250,000.[8] Critics of such studies usually point out the difficulty of holding the quality of services constant when estimating costs. However, the fact that these studies almost invariably find the range of maximum efficiency to be considerably less than the size of our big cities suggests that until evidence is produced to the contrary, the burden of proof lies with the defenders of the big city.

Finally, it is pertinent to note the conclusion drawn by participants at a conference—sponsored by the International Economic Association—in response to the question, "How large must a successful growth point be?" E. A. G. Robinson reports:

> The general sense of our discussions was that the minimum size of growth point that experience had shown to be successful was nearer to a population of 100,000 than to one of 10,000, and that even 100,000 was more likely to be an underestimate than an overestimate. It must be large enough to provide efficiently the main services of education, medical facilities, banking, shopping facilities. . . . Above all, it must be large enough both to provide an efficient infrastructure of public utility services, and to permit the early and progressive growth of external economies for its local industries.[9]

In other words, though it is agreed that small towns rarely make viable growth centers, the intermediate-sized city often does have the necessary conditions.

The foregoing discussion suggests that encouraging (or at least not discouraging) migration from lagging areas may be coupled with a growth-center policy based on external economies in cities in the 200,000 to 750,000 population range. Of course, these are rough indicators, not magic numbers, and the limits could be made sufficiently flexible to accommodate cities in the range from around 50,000 to 1 million or somewhat higher. Some observers have proposed that the solution to finding an optimum city size consists of finding the "point at which the economies of scale (or agglomeration) are equalled or exceeded by the diseconomies."[10] Although measurement of these variables is not a realistic prospect for the foreseeable future, the formulation of the problem in this manner is not quite correct. Even if expansion of a big city yielded a positive net social product, it would be preferable to have the expansion take place in an intermediate-sized city if the net social product were even greater there. The case for the intermediate-sized city is based on considerable evidence that it has most of the external economies of a big city but that it has not yet become a generator of significant external diseconomies.[11]

The emphasis that is given here to the development of intermediate cities as the principal focus for a national regional policy is based not only on the job-growth potential of these cities but also on the fact that problems related to their growth are still amenable to solution. The massive renewal needs of large metropolitan areas can still be avoided by careful planning in growth centers. Unless the government knows what places are going to grow, it can provide public facilities only after the demand has appeared. If there is planned growth of a relatively few centers, then they can be provided with an integrated and coherent system of public facilities in advance of the demand. Of course, it is not necessary that a growth center be limited to one city. A system of cities or towns linked by adequate transportation and communications might serve as well or better. Such a system could take the form of a cluster of urban centers or a development axis.

While growth centers may provide new opportunities for urban growth and employment for migrants from rural areas, they nevertheless are inadequate by themselves to solve either rural or urban poverty. Part of the solution to poverty must come from investments in human resources, the topic of the next section.

INVESTMENT IN HUMAN RESOURCES

One of the major developments in economics during the 1960s was the immense attention devoted to the significance of investment in human resources, or, as some would have it, human capital. Indeed, it now seems almost incredible that at the outset of the decade so little work had been done in this field. It now is apparent that among the factors that contribute to economic growth, the quality of the human input ranks very high. Conversely, one of the principal factors retarding the development of lagging regions is a relative deficiency in human-resource development. The lack is particularly evident in areas that have not experienced economic development, as contrasted with declining industrial areas that are in need of conversion of economic activities and readaptation of the labor force. These points have been developed at considerable length by the author elsewhere.[12]

The disadvantages that lagging areas encounter because of deficiencies in the health, education, and training of the labor force are familiar. However, lack of investment in human resources also has adverse effects on the political and business leadership of these areas. Although especially vigorous political and business leadership is needed if improvements are to be made in social and economic problems, "each of the essential elements in the leadership-technical-expert pattern tend to be relatively weak in distressed areas. The political leadership is often inbred, weak, and factionalized to the point of near paralysis. A dearth of alternative opportunities combined with decades of selective outmigration have removed young, dedicated, well-educated, and well-motivated men and women whose views extend beyond limited local horizons."[13] Entrepreneurship in lagging areas "has been diluted over the years by the dissolution or relocation of stronger local firms that, whatever their faults in 'milking' their business and community, nevertheless retained strong local ties and supplied civic direction at critical junctures." To the extent that new firms are attracted, their managers tend to be persons of brief tenure in branch plants of national firms or else marginal operators dependent on the favor of local politicians. In either case the newcomers have little political impact, and they frequently endeavor to retain their ties with other areas of the country. Finally, technicians employed in lagging areas "are often underpaid, substandard professionals more akin in quality and outlook to local civil servants than to professional staff found in metropolitan communities. The occasional capable elected official finds himself seriously handicapped by the absence of technicians qualified to seek out federal and private outside capital and to design and implement effective programs."[14]

Evidence that the most fundamental problem of lagging areas is underinvestment in human resources is perhaps best indicated by the high rate of return migration that occurs when new plants locate in these places. As one study of this phenomenon concludes, "More local people could be at work, at the expense of immigrants, if they had had the necessary minimum education or training. . . . That more were not hired brings up some pointed questions about education and skills in general."[15]

In many cases inadequate investment in human resources has occurred not only because local funds were inadequate but also because funds that were available have been squandered on attempts to attract industry. Instead of building better schools and using public amenities to attract firms, there has been a pronounced tendency to extend financial inducements directly to firms and to let the schools wait. In many cases, this has been an unwise reallocation of funds. These new firms usually have not provided many good new jobs and often have burdened the community with new demands on services without contributing much to finance them.

Realization of the dangers in trying to subsidize foot-loose and often marginal firms still has not overcome reluctance to upgrade human resources in many places. Because of the selective nature of outmigration, many communities know that better health facilities and better schools will only lead to an accelerated exodus of young people. There is something to be said for the people in relatively poor regions not wanting to see the payoff from their investment in mobile human beings go to relatively prosperous areas. Under these conditions poor regions are justified in asking the nation as a whole to support investment in their people, although public works and business-oriented programs, so favored in regional legislation, are difficult to justify because of better alternatives in regions with greater external economies.

Public Investment in Areas of Viable Commercial Agriculture

It should also be pointed out that many areas that are in "decline" in terms of net outmigration have adequate investments in human resources. In particular, it is difficult to lump together areas where commercial agriculture is still a source of viable employment

133

but where considerable outmigration is occurring, such as the Great Plains and Cornbelt, with lagging areas like central Appalachia, southern Texas, the southern Atlantic coastal plains, and the Mississippi Delta. Human investment in areas of viable commercial agriculture generally has been sufficient to provide education and health and to develop desirable work habits for preparing migrants from these areas for economic opportunities in other areas. These migrants have provided net contributions to the cities, and consequently their migration has represented a rural subsidy for urban development.

Even though these areas of viable commercial agriculture have a high degree of human-resource investment relative to rural poverty areas, it nevertheless cannot be denied that they have problems. This is particularly true in the Great Plains. For example, the population of the plains has a relatively high proportion of older persons, and it is often difficult to maintain essential services for widely dispersed people. On the other hand, there is very little poverty; in addition to savings and farm income, there is considerable income from the federal government in the form of farm subsidies and Social Security benefits. There also are viable small cities in these areas, though their size may restrict their development to that of service centers rather than of genuine growth centers capable of checking outmigration.

Perhaps the most important consideration concerning investment in the communities in the Great Plains and other areas of viable commercial agriculture with declining populations is the amount of social capital present in these towns and cities. These communities, in contrast with many of those in lagging areas, have well-developed infrastructures, high investment in social overhead capital, and generally desirable social organization. This social investment has been effective in preparing citizens who are well accepted in urban areas, and the deterioration of this social investment represents a loss to society. The crucial question here is whether public and private investment in these rural communities will save more social capital from deterioration than an equivalent investment in growth centers will produce in new capital. Research to date has not adequately examined this question, but the amount of social capital that could be saved by new investment may justify some public investment in these rural communities, particularly in areas where larger growth centers do not exist. Considerable research in this area is needed to determine priorities for public investment. Further directions for future research are analyzed in the next section.

DIRECTIONS FOR FUTURE RESEARCH

The complexities involved in alternative rural and urban growth strategies are of course too great to be dealt with completely in the scope of this paper. Moreover, further progress in this area requires a great deal of new information. For example, it is essential that a greater research effort be devoted to the economic and social trade-offs involved between migration of workers to jobs and efforts to move jobs to workers, especially when the workers in question are living in areas that have been lagging in terms of income and/or employment opportunities. There have been numerous studies of migration patterns, as well as of the adaptation of migrants from rural areas to urban places. Yet we know remarkably little about what it would have taken for these migrants to have remained at home, or about how many rural workers are at the margin with respect to migration and what would in fact induce them to migrate. Indeed, we know very little generally about the location preference patterns under various conditions of the persons who are supposed to be the object of rural-development policies.

A great deal of research related to the growth-center notion has not been very helpful, because although it has analyzed the agglomeration process in terms of external economies, it has failed to spell out how beneficial spread effects may actually be transmitted to lagging hinterlands. Growth-center theory and policy also have tended to focus on infrastructure investment in the narrow sense and have thereby diverted attention away from the critical health, education, and social problems that characterize most lagging regions.

Future growth-center research should give less emphasis to the promotion of growth in lagging areas and give greater attention to criteria for choosing viable intermediate urban centers; and it should put more stress on the manpower aspects of migration and of commuting to intermediate cities.

There is a limited but varied body of evidence suggesting that many persons in lagging areas would not mind moving—and might even prefer to move—to intermediate-sized cities not too distant from home. The Department of Labor recently carried out a number of labor-mobility demonstration projects in which a number of other agencies cooperated. In addition, the Employment Assistance Program of the Bureau of Indian Affairs has an ongoing program to aid in the voluntary relocation of Indians from reservations to urban areas. These limited undertakings have indicated that while it may be true that a poor worker may not want to move if this simply means being thrust into an alien environment, he frequently is well-disposed toward moving if he can receive comprehensive moving assistance, including training and help in finding a job; help in finding housing and in making contacts with schools and religious and social groups; and general assistance in adapting to an urban environment. More pilot projects and research need to be devoted to discovering the opportunities potentially available in migration to intermediate-sized cities.

In the light of 1970 census data, it appears that the gap between rural and urban areas narrowed somewhat during the 1960s, with fewer counties losing population during the 1960s (45%) than during the 1950s (50%). Much of the improved retention rate in rural areas, however, can be attributed to greater retention in the open country and in small towns under 500 population. Overall, larger nonmetropolitan cities (5,000–50,000 population) experienced only limited improvement. Undoubtedly there will be a new flood of recommendations for subsidies to attract economic activity to lagging, and for the most part rural, parts of the country. However, when marginal firms do locate in lagging rural areas, a high proportion of the new jobs often goes to persons who once migrated from the area but return to put their skills to work in their home community. Indeed, this phenomenon—which itself needs more study—clearly illustrates that the real problem of lagging areas is underinvestment in human resources rather than migration as such, which is more a symptom than a cause of distress.

There are, of course, many persons in lagging rural areas whose prospects for either local employment or for retraining and migration are not bright. For example, an unemployed or severely underemployed coal miner in Appalachia or a farmer in the Mississippi Delta who is fifty-five years old is not likely to find much solace from such efforts. On the other hand, evidence from both the United

States and other countries indicates that efforts to force-feed the economic development of large lagging areas are not only inefficient, but also largely ineffective. Those firms that are induced to locate in lagging areas are usually marginal in nature; they pay low wages and often will move on when a better subsidy presents itself. Nevertheless, there will always be marginal firms, and they may have an important role to play in giving employment to immobile persons in lagging areas—though marginal firms gravitate toward these areas even without subsidies. Cooperatives may also be useful in providing employment for these persons; the recent research of Marshall and Godwin should provide useful insights into this neglected approach.[16] In any event, much more realistic and thorough research needs to be undertaken on the matching of marginal economic activities with marginal workers who are unlikely to find any other kinds of employment.

Of course, there are rural areas that have given evidence of recent growth despite years of decline. It would be instructive to identify multicounty rural areas that have exhibited rapid growth in population and economic activity and to analyze the reasons for this growth (northwestern Arkansas is a good example). The aim of this research would be not only to identify why certain places grew, but to seek more general growth factors that may be applicable to other rural areas as well as the conditions under which they may be successfully applied. Research in this regard should concentrate on the nature and significance of the concept of rural industry. For example, there is evidence that in recent years manufacturing and other economic activities have grown at a more rapid rate in rural areas than in the country as a whole.[17] But is this "rural industry" really located for the most part in rural hinterlands or near Standard Metropolitan Statistical Areas, in effect being attracted by the SMSA's rather than anything specifically rural? For example, a Westinghouse plant employing eight hundred persons will soon be located in rural Williamson County, Texas; but it is probable that Austin, Texas, in neighboring Travis County, is the real pole of attraction in this case. What obviously would be required in this case and similar cases around the country would be an analysis of (1) the reasons for locating the relevant plants where they are and (2) the places of residence of persons employed in these plants. It may be that distinctions between rural and urban industry may in fact prove meaningless.

At present, manpower legislation and regional-development legislation are bifurcated, to the detriment of both. Much more understanding is needed of how they can be coherently integrated. Research possibilities along this line are abundant. Not only is there a need to examine specific policies and projects, but the whole question of the regionalization of the country for planning purposes must be considered. For example, should development regions be defined primarily on the basis of their low income and high unemployment, as is now the case? Or should regions be defined to include promising growth centers as well as poverty areas, so that problems and opportunities can be dealt with in a common planning framework? Perhaps it would be particularly instructive to investigate the programs of the Appalachian Regional Commission, which at this writing seems assured of a four-year extension. Recent congressional response has been so positive toward the Appalachian program that it clearly stands out as the most popular of the Great Society programs. What is most needed at this point concerning the Appalachian experience is a thorough and disinterested study of the nature and significance of the planning that has been carried out by the relevant states and multicounty district organizations. In particular, we need to know: (1) Do planning goals correspond to the most important needs of the areas in question? (2) Are federal, state, and local programs and projects being effectively coordinated? (3) What are the principal problems being encountered in planning formulation and implementation, and how are they being dealt with? (4) To what extent is the Appalachian experience a model for the rest of the country? (5) What relevance does Appalachian experience have for revenue-sharing with the states? (6) To what extent are the disadvantaged benefiting from the program?

The last question is especially critical in the present context. It is universally acknowledged that the popularity of the Appalachian program rests in large degree on the fact that it works through existing institutions. Federal programs in Appalachia that have seemed a threat to the power structure have met with considerable resistance. It is possible that "good" programs acceptable to the power structure may have a more realistic chance of helping the disadvantaged than "better" programs that are unacceptable to the power structure. However, the issue is by no means clear and will not be in the absence of thorough research.

These proposals are, of course, far from exhausting even the broad needs for further research on the problems of people in lagging rural areas and related problems of metropolitan central cities. They do indicate, however, a need to abandon any suggestion that problems of a local or regional nature can be dealt with as though they are isolated from a national system of forces.

NOTES

1. U.S. Department of Commerce, Economic Development Administration, *Program Evaluation: The Economic Development Administration Growth Center Strategy* (Washington, D.C.: U.S. Government Printing Office, February 1972), p. v.
2. See Niles M. Hansen, *Rural Poverty and the Urban Crisis* (Bloomington, Ind.: Indiana University Press, 1970), pp. 240–48, and *Intermediate-Size Cities As Growth Centers* (New York: Praeger, 1971).
3. Brian J. L. Berry, "Labor Market Participation and Regional Potential," *Growth and Change*, vol. 1, no. 4 (October 1970), p. 9.
4. Wilbur R. Thompson, *A Preface to Urban Economics* (Baltimore, Md.: Johns Hopkins Press, 1965), p. 24.
5. G. M. Neutze, *Economic Policy and the Size of Cities* (New York: Augustus M. Kelley, 1967), pp. 163, 109–18.
6. Colin Clark, "The Economic Functions of a City in Relation to Its Size," *Econometrica*, vol. 13, no. 2 (April 1945), pp. 97–113.
7. Werner Hirsch, "The Supply of Urban Public Services," in *Issues in Urban Economics*, ed. Harvey S. Perloff and Lowdon Wingo, Jr. (Baltimore, Md.: Johns Hopkins Press, 1968), pp. 509–11.
8. Gordon C. Cameron, "Growth Areas, Growth Centres and Regional Conversion," *Scottish Journal of Political Economy*, vol. 17, no. 1 (February 1970), pp. 24–25.
9. E. A. G. Robinson, "Introduction," in *Backward Areas in Advanced Countries*, ed. E. A. G. Robinson (New York: St. Martin's Press, 1969), p. xvi.
10. D. J. Reynolds, *Economics, Town Planning and Traffic* (London: Institute of Economic Affairs, 1966), p. 21.
11. Even with respect to amenities, one must be careful not to overestimate the advantages of the big city. New York may offer three hundred plays, concerts, and recitals in a given week, while a city of 600,000 may offer only twenty-five. Though the overall quality may be better in New York, the average person still has time only to take in a fraction of

the offerings in the intermediate-sized city. Though there is a wider range of choice in New York, it would be difficult to argue that the cultural advantages of living there are twelve times greater than in the intermediate-sized city. Modern home-entertainment equipment also has served to lessen the importance of living in a big city.

12. See Niles M. Hansen, *French Regional Planning* (Bloomington, Ind.: Indiana University Press, 1968), chaps. 1, 7, and 11, and *Rural Poverty and the Urban Crisis.*

13. Melvin R. Levin, *Community and Regional Planning* (New York: Praeger, 1969), p. 203.

14. Ibid., p. 204.

15. Irwin Gray, "Employment Effect of a New Industry in a Rural Area," *Monthly Labor Review*, vol. 92, no. 6 (June 1969), p. 29.

16. Ray Marshall and Lamond Godwin, *Cooperatives and Rural Poverty in the South* (Baltimore, Md.: Johns Hopkins Press, 1971).

17. Claude C. Haren, "Rural Industrial Growth in the 1960's," *American Journal of Agricultural Economics*, vol. 52, no. 3 (August 1970), pp. 431–37.

Lewis and Clark College - Watzek Library
HN65 .B72   wmain
Brinkman, George Lo/The development of r

3 5209 00429 9737